HAPPY RETIREMENT

Fun Things to Do from Home Hobbies to Wild Freedom

The Comprehensive Guide for Men, Women, and Everyone
Planning a Joyful Future

Leon Simonds

ISBN: 9798863179216

Foreword

Welcome, my dear reader, to a conversation that could change the course of your retirement, one that's as friendly and inclusive as a heartfelt chat with an old friend. In these pages, we'll embark on a journey that promises not only to guide you but also to stand beside you as you navigate the exciting waters of retirement.

As we begin, let me assure you that this book isn't just about dollars and cents; it's about dreams and aspirations, about the colorful tapestry of your life that's waiting to be woven anew. It's about recognizing that retirement is not a destination but a joyful voyage.

In these uncertain times, we understand that you might be feeling a mix of emotions— perhaps a tad anxious, a bit excited, or even a touch uncertain. That's why we approach this journey with empathy, knowing that every retiree's path is unique. You're not alone in these feelings; many have walked this path before, and we're here to share their stories and wisdom with you.

But above all, we want you to know that this book is here to encourage you, to fan the flames of your curiosity, and to inspire you to take action. Your retirement is a blank canvas waiting for your vibrant strokes of creativity, and we believe in your ability to paint a masterpiece.

So, dear reader, let's embark on this adventure together—one filled with friendly guidance, empathetic understanding, inclusive wisdom, and the unwavering encouragement to create a retirement that's nothing short of inspirational. Your journey starts now, and the destination? Well, that's something we'll discover together.

Table of Contents

Introduction

The New Definition of Retirement

In the not-so-distant past, retirement was often seen as the finish line—a place where the daily grind ended and the pursuit of leisure began. But let's chat about something quite exciting: the new definition of retirement.

You see, my friend, retirement today is about so much more than just slowing down. It's about rewiring your life for joy, purpose, and personal fulfillment. And guess what? You're not alone in this journey; millions around the world are redefining retirement just like you.

Here's the thing, retirement isn't a one-size-fits-all deal. It's as diverse as the people it embraces. Some retire to travel the world, while others stay closer to home, immersing themselves in community projects. Some pick up new hobbies, while others revisit cherished passions.

In this era of possibilities, your retirement can be a fusion of everything you love and aspire to be. It's a time for you to bloom, to become the author of your own adventure, and to discover the magic that life still holds.

And you know what? It's completely okay if you're feeling a mix of emotions—excitement, uncertainty, nostalgia. That's part of the journey. Embrace it, because it's all part of the beautiful tapestry of retirement.

So, let's embark on this journey of rediscovery together. Remember, there's no right or wrong way to do this, only your way. We're here to encourage and inspire you every step of the way.

Opportunities in Retirement

Rediscovery of Self: Embracing the Lifelong Journey

In retirement, rediscovering yourself is not just an abstract concept; it's a practical and deeply enriching journey that everyone can embark upon. Let's explore how to make this journey tangible and transformative:

Embracing Self-Discovery as a Lifelong Journey

✓ Start by setting aside dedicated time for self-reflection. Create a journal where you can jot down your thoughts, memories, and ideas about what truly excites you.

✓ Reach out to old friends and family members for conversations about your shared experiences. Sometimes, revisiting your past can provide valuable insights into your core interests.

Reflecting on Your Passions, Interests, and Dreams

✓ Make a list of activities and hobbies you've enjoyed throughout your life. What were you doing when you felt the most alive and engaged? These moments often hold clues to your true passions.

✓ Consider taking personality assessments or career aptitude tests. While they might sound like something for the younger crowd, these tools can shed light on your innate strengths and interests.

Unearthing Hidden Talents and Aspirations

✓ Experiment with new activities and experiences. Whether it's learning to play a musical instrument, trying your hand at painting, or taking up a new sport, exploration is key to uncovering hidden talents.

✓ Seek out local clubs, groups, or classes related to your interests. These social connections can be a great source of motivation and can help you hone your skills.

Inspiring Stories of Retirees Who Embarked on Incredible Journeys of Self-Renewal

✓ Read books, and articles, or watch documentaries about retirees who reinvented themselves in retirement. Learning from others' experiences can provide practical insights and motivation.

✓ Connect with local retirees who have embraced new adventures. Their stories are often a treasure trove of practical advice and inspiration. Attend community events, join clubs, and actively seek out these mentors.

Remember, self-discovery is not a destination but an ongoing journey. It's about taking practical steps, trying new things, and embracing opportunities as they come your way. In this journey, you're not alone; you're part of a community of like-minded individuals who are also exploring and growing. So, take that first step today, and let the adventure of self-discovery in retirement begin.

Unscheduled Time – A Gift

One of the most profound gifts that retirement bestows upon you is unscheduled time. It's like receiving a beautifully wrapped present every day, with the freedom to choose how you want to unwrap it. Here's how you can make the most of this priceless gift:

Recognizing the Value of Unscheduled Time in Retirement

✓ **Shift your perspective:** View unscheduled time not as an empty void but as a canvas ready to be filled with the colors of your desires and dreams. It's an opportunity to reclaim your time and craft your days intentionally.

✓ **Embrace freedom:** Liberating yourself from the constraints of a rigid schedule allows you to savor the simple pleasures of life. Enjoy that leisurely morning coffee, take spontaneous walks, or get lost in a good book without the pressure of a ticking clock.

Shifting from a Clock-Driven Life to a Purpose-Driven One

✓ **Reflect on your values:** Take time to ponder what truly matters to you. What are the values that define your life? Use this newfound time to align your daily activities with these core values.

✓ **Set intentions:** Instead of being driven solely by routine, set clear intentions for your days. Whether it's dedicating time to a hobby you love, volunteering for a cause close to your heart, or spending quality moments with loved ones, intentions guide your unscheduled time toward meaningful experiences.

Embracing Spontaneity and the Beauty of Unstructured Days

✓ **Say yes to adventure:** Allow yourself to be open to spontaneous adventures and opportunities. It could be exploring a nearby trail you've never ventured onto or joining an impromptu gathering of friends.

✓ **Embrace downtime:** Understand that it's perfectly okay to do nothing at times. In the hustle and bustle of our previous lives, we often overlook the simple joy of doing absolutely nothing. Use unscheduled time to savor moments of pure relaxation.

Remember, unscheduled time is a precious gift waiting to be unwrapped and savored. It's an opportunity to rediscover the simple joys of life, pursue your passions, and create a purpose-driven retirement. So, let's celebrate the gift of unscheduled time!

How to Use This Book

Your User-Friendly Guide to Retirement

Navigating a book about retirement should be as enjoyable as planning your retirement itself. That's why we've designed "Happy Retirement" to be your friendly companion on this remarkable journey. It's a guide that fits everyone, regardless of where you are on your retirement path.

Whether you're a meticulous planner or someone who loves to go with the flow, this book is designed with you in mind. It's user-friendly, offering a range of insights and advice suitable for all types of retirees. Whether you're approaching retirement with financial confidence or a few questions, our aim is to provide you with valuable information that empowers you to make informed decisions.

Chapters I and II: Money and Psychology

In Chapters I and II, we delve deep into the essential pillars of retirement—money and psychology. These chapters are your foundation, providing a solid understanding of financial planning, budgeting, and the psychological aspects of transitioning into retirement. You'll find a wealth of practical information to help you navigate the financial and emotional terrain of retirement.

A Roadmap for the "What to Do" Moments

But what about those moments when you wonder, "What should I do with all this unscheduled time?" That's where Chapters 3 to 8 come into play. These chapters are your treasure trove of ideas and recommendations, carefully curated to inspire and guide you when you're seeking new adventures and meaningful pursuits.

Discovering the Answers and Recommendations

- In **Chapter 3**, you'll explore a world of physical activities that promote health and vitality.

- **Chapter 4** unleashes your creativity through artistic expression and DIY projects.

- **Chapter 5** is your gateway to lifelong learning and intellectual pursuits.

- In **Chapter 6**, you'll discover the joy of community involvement and giving back.

- **Chapter 7** invites you to explore new horizons through travel and cultural immersion.

- Finally, **Chapter 8** is all about relaxation, mindfulness, and embracing serenity.

So, think of this book as your compass, guiding you through the intricate terrain ofetirement. Whether you're looking for financial wisdom, seeking the courage to embrace change, or craving inspiration for your next adventure, "Happy Retirement" is here to be your trusted companion.

As you embark on this transformative journey, know that you're never alone. You have the collective wisdom of countless retirees and the encouragement of an entire community behind you. So, let's turn the pages of your retirement adventure together and uncover the vibrant tapestry of life that awaits you.

Chapter 1: Smart Financial Lifestyle

"Whoever said money can't buy happiness didn't know where to shop!"

Chapter 1: Smart Financial Lifestyle

1.1 Financial Well-being

Welcome to the gateway of your smart financial lifestyle in retirement. As the author of this comprehensive guide, I bring decades of expertise in the field of retirement planning to assist you on this transformative journey. In this section, we'll embark on a journey that emphasizes inclusivity, empathy, and practical guidance while understanding the vital role of financial well-being in your retirement.

Understanding the Importance of Financial Well-being in Retirement

Retirement is a universal concept that spans diverse backgrounds and circumstances. It's important to recognize that financial well-being is a shared concern. This journey includes everyone, and I'm here to guide you.

It's natural to feel a range of emotions when it comes to financial well-being in retirement. Some may feel anxious, while others may be excited. I understand these feelings and approach this topic with empathy, knowing that your unique situation deserves understanding and support.

Beyond the abstract, let's get practical. Financial well-being isn't just about big numbers; it's about the day-to-day decisions and actions that shape your retirement. I'm here to provide actionable insights and guidance.

While understanding the importance of financial well-being can sometimes feel daunting, it's essential to remember that every step forward, no matter how small, brings you closer to a comfortable retirement. This section aims to encourage and empower you on this journey.

1.2 Current Financial State

Now, let's roll up our sleeves and get practical as we dive into the essential task of assessing your current financial situation.

Taking Stock of Your Assets, Income, and Expenses

Imagine sitting down with a trusted advisor, ready to tackle your financial situation over a cup of coffee. This process is designed to be approachable and inclusive because financial planning is for everyone.

Understanding that discussing finances can sometimes be challenging, rest assured that this process is about gaining clarity and planning for your future.

Let's get hands-on with some practical methods to help you assess your financial landscape:

1. **Create an Asset Inventory:** Start by listing all your assets, such as savings accounts, investments, real estate, and valuable possessions. Assign values to each asset to determine your total assets.

2. **Track Your Income:** Gather information on your sources of income, including pensions, Social Security, and any other earnings. Calculate your annual income and assess its stability.

3. **Budget Your Expenses:** Create a detailed budget that outlines your monthly expenses. This includes essentials like housing, food, utilities, and discretionary spending. Identify areas where you can potentially cut back to increase savings.

4. **Use Financial Software:** Consider using financial software or apps to streamline this process. They can help you track your expenses, categorize spending, and generate reports to see where your money is going.

Remember, this process empowers you; there's no judgment here. Every insight you gain brings you closer to financial confidence in retirement.

Calculating Your Retirement Savings and Investments

Imagine you're in a workshop, where complex financial topics are broken down into simple, practical steps.

This isn't just for financial experts; it's for everyone. Your journey to calculate your retirement savings and investments is a shared experience.

It's perfectly normal to have questions and concerns about your financial future. Rest assured, you're not alone in this journey, and support is readily available.

Now, let's roll up our sleeves and dive into the nitty-gritty. Here are some practical methods to help you calculate your retirement savings and investments:

1.   **Gather Investment Statements:** Collect statements from all your investment accounts, including 401(k)s, IRAs, stocks, and bonds. Summarize the current balances and note any fees or penalties for early withdrawals.

2.   **Calculate Future Value:** Utilize online retirement calculators or consult with a financial advisor to estimate the future value of your investments based on your current contributions and expected returns.

3.   **Review Pension and Social Security:** Contact your pension plan administrator and Social Security office to obtain estimates of your future benefits. Understand how these income sources will contribute to your retirement income.

4.   **Account for Inflation:** Adjust your savings and investment calculations for inflation to ensure your money retains its purchasing power in retirement.

Each calculation you make is a practical step toward your retirement goals. Your journey is unique, and every practical action you take brings you one step closer to the retirement you envision.

1.3 Financial Goals

Now that we've assessed your current financial situation, it's time to set clear financial goals for your retirement. In this section, we'll provide you with a practical roadmap for achieving your objectives.

Defining Your Retirement Goals and Aspirations

Imagine we're here to help you explore your retirement dreams in a straightforward manner. Our aim is to assist you in articulating your goals and aspirations:

✓ **Reflect on Your Passions:** Begin by considering what truly brings you joy. What are your passions and interests? Your retirement years offer a unique opportunity to delve deeper into these pursuits.

✓ **Consider Bucket List Items:** Take a moment to think about your bucket list. Whether it's traveling to new destinations, mastering a new hobby, or dedicating time to meaningful causes, jot down these aspirations.

✓ **Prioritize Your Values:** Identify the values that hold the most significance for you in retirement. Is it spending quality time with family, achieving financial security, or making a positive impact in your community? Your values will guide your goal-setting.

Creating a Roadmap for Achieving Your Financial Objectives

Now, let's translate these aspirations into actionable steps—a practical roadmap toward a fulfilling retirement:

✓ **Set Specific Goals:** Transform your aspirations into specific, measurable, and time-bound goals. For instance, if travel is on your list, specify your desired destination and set a timeline for the journey.

✓ **Calculate Costs:** Determine the financial implications of your goals. How much will your dream endeavors cost? This step ensures that your goals remain realistic and attainable.

✓ **Explore Income Sources:** Assess your potential sources of income in retirement, such as savings, investments, pensions, and Social Security. How will these sources support your goals?

✓ **Create a Savings Plan:** Develop a practical savings plan to fund your retirement objectives. Consider automating your savings to ensure consistency.

✓ **Review and Adjust:** Your financial roadmap is dynamic. Periodically review your progress and make adjustments as needed. Life may bring unexpected opportunities and challenges, so stay flexible.

This section is all about turning your retirement dreams into a tangible plan, helping you set goals that are meaningful and achievable. As you define your goals and chart your path, you're taking proactive steps toward realizing the retirement you've envisioned.

1.4 Retirement Budget

Now that you've set clear financial goals, it's time to delve into the art of budgeting for your retirement. In this section, we'll guide you through the process of crafting a retirement budget that ensures your financial well-being.

The Art of Budgeting in Retirement

Budgeting doesn't have to feel like a chore; it's a valuable tool that empowers you to manage your finances effectively during retirement.

- ✓ **Prioritize Financial Well-being:** We'll help you prioritize your financial well-being while maintaining a fulfilling retirement lifestyle.

- ✓ **Budgeting as Empowerment:** Budgeting isn't about restrictions; it's about making informed choices that align with your goals and values.

- ✓ **Tracking Your Expenses:** Learn practical techniques for tracking your expenses, giving you a clear understanding of where your money goes.

Allocating Resources for Essential Expenses, Leisure Activities, and Savings

Effective budgeting involves allocating your resources wisely to cover your essential expenses, enjoy leisure activities, and save for the future.

- ✓ **Essential Expenses:** We'll guide you on budgeting for essentials like housing, utilities, healthcare, and groceries, ensuring your basic needs are met.

- ✓ **Leisure Activities:** Discover how to budget for leisure activities, such as travel, hobbies, dining out, and entertainment, without compromising your financial security.

- ✓ **Prioritizing Savings:** We'll emphasize the importance of allocating a portion of your budget to savings, helping you build a financial cushion for unexpected events and future dreams.

By mastering the art of budgeting in retirement and strategically allocating your resources, you'll gain a sense of control and financial peace of mind. This section will empower you to make informed decisions about your finances, ensuring that your retirement lifestyle aligns with your aspirations and priorities.

1.5 Building and Protecting Your Retirement Nest Egg

Now that you have a clear financial roadmap and budget in place, let's focus on two important aspects: how to make your retirement savings grow and how to protect them. In this section, we'll explore simple strategies for growing your retirement savings and why it's crucial to have insurance and estate planning.

Growing Your Retirement Savings

Growing your retirement savings is like planting seeds that will grow into a big tree over time. Here are some simple ways to help your savings grow:

✓ **Investing Smartly:** Think of investing as a way to make your money work for you. We'll show you how to choose the right investments that have the potential to make your savings grow faster.

✓ **Spreading Your Money:** Just like you wouldn't put all your eggs in one basket, it's a good idea not to put all your money in one place. We'll explain how to spread your money across different investments to keep it safe and growing.

✓ **Adding Regularly:** Imagine adding a few dollars to your savings jar every week. Over time, those small additions can add up to a lot. We'll talk about the benefits of adding money to your retirement savings regularly.

By using these simple strategies, you can help your retirement savings grow steadily, like a tree getting taller year by year.

The Importance of Insurance and Estate Planning

Protecting your savings is like putting a fence around your garden to keep it safe. Here's why it's important:

✓ **Insurance Shield:** We'll explain how insurance can protect you from unexpected events, like health issues or accidents, that could affect your savings. It's like having an umbrella on a rainy day.

✓ **Planning for the Future:** Just like you make plans for a vacation, you need to plan for what happens to your savings in the future. Estate planning ensures your money goes where you want it to go when you're no longer around.

✓ **Leaving a Legacy:** Lastly, think of your savings as a gift you can leave for your loved ones or a cause you care about. We'll discuss how to make sure your savings benefit the people and things you care about most.

By understanding these simple ideas, you'll be better equipped to make your retirement savings grow and keep them safe for the future.

1.6 Smart Investing

Now, let's talk about another important topic: how to be smart with your money to ensure a secure future. In this section, we'll explore the world of investing and how to make wise choices for your financial well-being.

Exploring Investment Options and Strategies

Investing might sound like a big word, but it's like choosing where to plant your seeds to make your money grow. We'll break it down for you:

✓ **Different Investment Choices:** There are various ways to invest your money, such as stocks, bonds, or real estate. We'll explain each option in simple terms so you can decide which one suits you best.

✓ **Strategy Secrets:** Think of investment strategies as your game plan. We'll share straightforward strategies that can help you make the most of your investments, whether you want steady growth or are willing to take a bit more risk for potentially higher returns.

Diversification

Diversification is like not putting all your eggs in one basket. It means spreading your investments across different types of assets, like stocks, bonds, and real estate. This reduces the risk that one bad investment will have a big impact on your overall portfolio.

Asset Allocation

Imagine creating a recipe with the right mix of ingredients. Asset allocation involves deciding how much of your portfolio should be in different asset classes. It's like figuring out the right blend of flavors to make your meal delicious. Your mix depends on your financial goals and risk tolerance.

Dollar-Cost Averaging

Think of this as regularly investing a fixed amount of money, like making monthly deposits into your savings account. When prices are high, you buy fewer shares, and when prices are low, you buy more. Over time, this strategy can reduce the impact of market ups and downs on your investments.

Rebalancing

Picture a seesaw. As your investments grow or decline, the balance between different asset classes may shift. Rebalancing involves periodically adjusting your portfolio to maintain your desired asset allocation. It's like leveling the seesaw to keep it steady.

Buy and Hold

Imagine you've planted a sturdy tree sapling in your garden. You let it grow steadily over the years without constantly digging it up to check the roots. Buy and hold involves choosing quality investments and holding them for the long term, regardless of short-term market fluctuations.

Risk Management

Assess your risk tolerance and choose investments that align with it. If you're uncomfortable with significant fluctuations in your portfolio, consider investments with lower volatility, even if they offer potentially lower returns.

Educate Yourself

Knowledge is your compass in the investment world. Take the time to learn about the investments you're considering and stay informed about market trends and economic developments. Knowledge can empower you to make informed decisions.

By understanding these simple investment options and strategies, you can make informed decisions about how to grow your money wisely and create a secure financial future.

1.7 Debt Management

In this section, we'll talk about some practical tips and simple strategies to help you handle debt and ease financial worries during your retirement.

Tips for Debt Management in Retirement:

✓ **Know Your Debts:** Start by figuring out what you owe. This includes any money you've borrowed, like loans or credit card balances.

✓ **Pay High-Interest Debts First:** If you have debts with high interest rates, focus on paying them off sooner. This can save you money in the long run.

✓ **Set Money Aside:** Make a budget to ensure you have enough money to pay off your debts regularly. This helps you stay on track.

Strategies to Reduce Financial Stress:

✓ **Create an Emergency Fund:** Having some money set aside for unexpected expenses can bring peace of mind. It means you won't need to rely on credit if something unexpected comes up.

✓ **Cut Back Wisely:** Find ways to spend a little less in your daily life. Even small changes can make a difference in reducing financial stress.

✓ **Ask for Expert Advice:** Consider talking to financial experts who specialize in retirement planning and debt management. They can give you personalized advice based on your unique situation.

By using these straightforward debt management tips and stress-reduction strategies, you can work toward a more financially secure and enjoyable retirement.

1.8 Conclusion: Financial Confidence

As we conclude this chapter on financial savvy living, it's time to recognize the profound connection between financial well-being and your overall quality of life in retirement. This conclusion serves as a bridge, preparing you for the journey ahead with newfound confidence and empowerment, knowing that we've covered the essential financial aspects in this chapter.

The Interconnectedness of Financial and Overall Well-being

Consider your financial well-being as a vital component of your overall life satisfaction. It's like a well-balanced wheel on a bicycle, contributing to the smooth ride of your entire journey. In this section, we'll delve into how your financial choices impact your overall well-being, including your physical and emotional health.

Preparing for the Financial Journey Ahead with Confidence

With the financial foundation laid in this chapter, you're equipped to embark on your retirement journey with confidence. It's akin to setting sail on well-charted waters, knowing you possess the tools and understanding to navigate smoothly.

In the upcoming chapters, we'll explore various aspects of retirement living, from pursuing your passions and interests to nurturing your physical and psychological well-being. Each chapter will provide you with practical guidance and inspiration for leading a fulfilling and meaningful retirement life.

So, as you continue reading, remember that your financial well-being is an integral part of your retirement adventure. By embracing it with confidence and understanding its connection to your overall well-being, you're well-prepared to embark on a joyful and enriching retirement journey.

CHAPTER 1 ACTIVITY CHECKLIST
Smart Financial Lifestyle

Purpose: This checklist is designed to help you translate the insights and advice from this chapter into actionable steps, setting you on the path to a smarter financial lifestyle.

Getting Started:

✓ **Budget Basics:** Draft or refresh your monthly budget.

✓ **Income Insights:** List all current income sources.

✓ **Expense Examination:** Monitor and record your daily expenses for a week.

Savings & Investments:

✓ **Retirement Review:** Open or evaluate an existing retirement savings account.

✓ **Savings Strategy:** Set aside a specific percentage of your income for savings.

✓ **Investment Introduction:** Explore and learn about a new investment opportunity.

Debts & Liabilities:

✓ **Debt Details:** Make a comprehensive list of all outstanding debts.

✓ **Priority Payments:** Focus on clearing high-interest debts first.

✓ **Payment Plan:** Create a strategy to steadily reduce debts.

Insurance & Safety Nets:

✓ **Health Highlight:** Reassess the suitability of your health insurance plan.

✓ **Life Lookover:** Consider or review a life insurance policy.

✓ **Estate Exploration:** Begin or review the basics of estate planning.

Reflective Corner:

1. **Insight Inspiration:** What financial discovery or realization stood out this week?

2. **Priority Perspective:** Which financial area (savings, debt, insurance) requires your immediate focus?

Bonus Action:

✓ **Financial Workshop:** Register for a financial workshop, whether in-person or online.

Note: Revisit this checklist periodically to track your progress and ensure you stay on course with your financial goals.

Chapter 2:
Retirement Psychology

"Retirement: Monday mornings never
felt so good!"

Chapter 2: Retirement Psychology

2.1 Emotional Transition

About Feelings

So, you're retiring, huh? First off, congrats! It's a big step. But I bet a flurry of feelings are racing through your heart right now. Excited? Scared? A mix of both? It's completely normal. Retirement isn't just about leaving your job; it's about entering a new chapter. And just like any big change, it can come with a roller coaster of emotions.

The Many Shades of Retirement Emotions

Retirement isn't a one-size-fits-all experience. Some days you might feel on top of the world, eager to take on new hobbies or travel. On other days, the quiet might feel a bit too... well, quiet. Maybe you'll miss the routine, your colleagues, or the sense of purpose your job gave you.

It's Okay to Feel... Everything!

It's okay to have mixed feelings. Joy, uncertainty, relief, fear – they're all part of the journey. Remember, it's a transition, not an endpoint. The beauty of this phase is that it's moldable. You get to shape it the way you want.

Tips to Navigate Your Emotions

- ✓ **Talk it out:** Chat with friends or family, join a retirement group, or even consider counselling. Sometimes, just voicing your feelings makes a world of difference.

- ✓ **Stay active:** Physical activity isn't just good for the body; it's great for the soul too. A short walk or a new dance class can lift your spirits.

- ✓ **Keep a journal:** Penning down your thoughts can be therapeutic. Plus, it's a great way to track your journey and the changes in your emotions over time.

- ✓ **Rediscover old passions or find new ones:** Maybe it's that guitar you stopped playing or a new hobby like photography. Dive in!

Remember, it's okay to ask for help: If you're feeling too overwhelmed, there's no shame in seeking professional advice or guidance.

So, as you take this new step, remember that all your feelings are valid. Embrace them, understand them, and use them as a guide to make this chapter of life truly yours. Cheers to new beginnings!

2.2 Identity and Self-Worth

Let's Dive Into Who You Are

You've probably been introduced or even introduced yourself with the line, "I work at [Job Title] at [Company]," for years, maybe even decades. Now that you're retired, you might be wondering, "Who am I without my job?" The journey of rediscovering yourself and understanding your value beyond work is what we're diving into today.

The Label Game

Throughout our lives, we wear so many labels: parent, partner, friend, and, of course, our job titles. While these labels help give context, they aren't the entirety of who we are. But sometimes, it's easy to get lost in one label, especially a label you've worn proudly for years.

You Are So Much More!

Your job was a part of your life, but it wasn't ALL of you. Think of all the roles you've played, all the hobbies you've had, all the laughs and stories you've shared. That richness is your true identity.

Rebuilding the Picture of You

- ✓ **Reconnect with old passions:** Remember those things you loved doing but never had time for? Maybe it's painting, reading, or dancing. Now's the time!
- ✓ **New adventures, new you:** Ever wanted to learn pottery? Or how about sailing? Trying something new can be a fun way to add more layers to your identity.
- ✓ **Share your story:** Talk to family or friends, share memories, or even start a blog. Celebrate every version of yourself.
- ✓ **Help others:** Often, we discover the most about ourselves when we're helping others. Volunteer, mentor, or simply be there for someone.
- ✓ **Self-reflection:** Take moments for yourself. Whether it's through meditation, journaling, or a quiet morning cup of coffee, connect with your inner self.

Friend, as you step into this new phase, remember that retirement is just another label. Peel it back, and there's a world of experiences, memories, and dreams that make you the wonderful person you are. Embrace the journey of self-discovery and celebrate yourself every step of the way. Cheers to the amazing you!

2.3 Purpose & Meaning

Adventurer of Life!

Retirement doesn't mean you've reached the end of the road; in fact, it's the beginning of an exciting new chapter! Ever had that itch, wondering, "What's my purpose now?" or "What's this chapter of life all about?" Let's dive into this together.

The Great "Why?"

Throughout life, we often chase goals: get that job, buy that house, raise a family. Once you retire, the scenery changes, but the journey doesn't end. Instead, it shifts from the "What" and "How" to the big "Why".

Discovering Your New "Why"

✓ **Passions Revived:** Those hobbies or causes you shelved due to work or life commitments? Dust them off! They could be the key to your newfound purpose.

✓ **Give Back:** Whether it's mentoring, volunteering, or even just lending an ear to a friend in need, helping others can fill your heart and days with purpose.

✓ **Learn, Learn, Learn:** Dive into books, courses, or even travel. Discover topics that ignite your heart and brain. Who knows? Maybe there's a subject out there just waiting to become your new passion.

✓ **Legacy Building:** How do you want to be remembered? Maybe it's by sharing stories with grandkids, writing a book, or creating something for your community. Think big, dream bigger!

✓ **Mindfulness and the Moment:** Sometimes, purpose isn't grand. It's in the small moments – watching a sunrise, tending to your garden, or savoring a cup of tea. Cherish these moments.

Dear friend, retirement is like getting a brand-new notebook. Each page is waiting to be filled with your stories, adventures, and memories. Whether you pen down epic tales or jot down quiet reflections, remember, it's your narrative. Your purpose is as unique as your journey. So, go ahead, start writing, and let every page be a testament to the beautiful chapters still to come. Happy discovering!

2.4 Change & Loss

Change. It's like the constant ebb and flow of the ocean, sometimes gentle, other times rough, but always present. And retirement? Well, it brings its own tide of changes. The routines you were so used to, the people you saw every day, the tasks that defined many of your hours—they shift. And that shift, my friend, can sometimes leave a little hole that feels a lot like loss.

It's okay to feel the weight of that void. Perhaps you're missing the buzz of the 9-to-5, the camaraderie with coworkers, or even the challenges that once felt like a burden. It's a bit like moving away from a town you've lived in for years. You'll miss the familiarity, the neighbors, and even that old coffee shop around the corner.

But remember, every ending brings the promise of a new beginning. When one door closes, another one surely opens. The key is to look forward and not get stuck staring at the closed door for too long. While it's essential to allow yourself to grieve, it's equally important to search for the new opportunities that lie ahead.

Embrace new routines. Maybe it's time to pick up that guitar you always wanted to learn or start a garden in your backyard. Meet new people or even reconnect with old friends. Dive into a hobby or take a class you've been eyeing. There's a world of possibilities out there.

But here's a small secret: The waves of change might try to push you around, but you're the captain of your ship. Steer it in the direction of your dreams, ride out the storms, and seek out new horizons. The ocean of retirement can be vast and unpredictable, but it's also filled with potential and beauty.

Here's to navigating the waters with hope and courage!

2.5 Social Ties

You know that warm, fuzzy feeling you get when you catch up with an old friend over a cup of coffee? Or the joy of laughing out loud at a family gathering? That's the magic of social ties. Throughout our lives, we're like little spiders spinning webs of connections. These connections – friends, family, neighbors, even the friendly barista at your favorite coffee spot – add color, warmth, and depth to our world.

Now, retirement can sometimes shuffle the deck a bit. You might not see those work buddies as often, and the daily chit-chat by the water cooler becomes a thing of the past. It's natural to feel a void, but hey, it's not the end of the story!

Think of this time as an opportunity. Maybe it's the universe nudging you to expand your social circle or dive deeper into the relationships you already cherish. Why not join a local club or group that aligns with your interests? It could be a book club, a hiking group, or even a dance class (shake a leg and make friends, win-win!).

And don't forget the wonders of technology. With video calls and online communities, staying connected has never been easier. Reach out, send a message, make that call. Let someone know you're thinking of them.

Plus, let's be real for a moment. Some alone time is pretty awesome, too. It gives you space to reflect, rejuvenate, and rediscover parts of yourself. But balancing that with social interactions is the secret sauce to a flavorful life.

So, get out there (or stay in with a phone in hand)! Build bridges, strengthen bonds, create new ones, and cherish the old. After all, our web of connections is what makes life rich and vibrant. Cheers to weaving the tapestry of human connections even tighter in retirement!

2.6 Balanced Lifestyle

Let's chat about seesaws. Remember playing on them as a kid? Life's a bit like a seesaw. Too much weight on one side? Things go wonky. In retirement, the challenge is balancing time, not weight.

With the 9-to-5 hustle behind you, it's a dreamy thought: "I've got all this free time, now what?" It's a golden chance, but it's all about striking the right balance.

Sure, you could strum away on that guitar, dive into books that've been waiting for your attention, or even take up painting. But then, don't forget to enjoy those calm mornings, sipping tea and just...being.

Variety? It's your best pal now. Some days, you'll be engrossed in a hobby, and on others, maybe you'll just saunter in the park or chat with a friend over the fence.

Ever thought about being spontaneous? Like, out-of-the-blue visiting your grandkids or maybe trying out that trendy café? It's your time, surprise yourself!

Speaking of time, cherish those quiet moments. There's magic in stillness. And honestly, every now and then, embracing the joy of doing absolutely nothing? It's golden.

Now, if you're thinking, "But how do I find all these cool things to do?" That's where this book waltzes in! It's like your treasure map, guiding you to things you can explore, experience, and enjoy. Let's find those hidden gems together, shall we?

The key takeaway? It's all about rhythm. Swing to your own beat. Retirement's your dance floor, so make every move count. Find your balance, and when in doubt, turn to the next page of this book for a sprinkle of inspiration.

2.7 Mental Health

Okay, let's sit down and have a heart-to-heart. Remember those times when you'd feel blue for no reason or a little foggy up there in the brain department? Those moments aren't exclusive to our younger days. Mental health is important at every stage, and in retirement, it's a topic we ought to give a cozy spotlight.

First things first: it's okay not to be okay sometimes. Everyone has off days. It's like weather inside us: some days are sunny, others might be a bit cloudy, and occasionally, there's a full-blown storm.

With more free time, your mind might sometimes wander into the alleys of the past or worry about the unpredictable future. Maybe you'll miss the rush of deadlines or the chatter of colleagues. Or perhaps, you'll cherish the tranquillity but occasionally feel a smidge isolated.

Here's the good news: You've got the power to shape your mindset! Feeling connected can be as simple as joining a club, taking a class, or just strolling to the local store for some chit-chat. Heck, even calling up an old friend for a random laugh-a-thon can do wonders!

For the more cloudy days, it might help to embrace activities that center you. Think meditation, deep breathing, or even just listening to the rhythm of raindrops. And hey, if things ever feel too heavy, remember that seeking professional help or counseling isn't a sign of weakness. It's like calling a plumber when the sink's acting up. Sometimes, we just need a bit of expert help to clear the pipes.

This chapter's all about nurturing that beautiful brain of yours. Keep it healthy, keep it lively, and remember, it's okay to ask for help when the fog gets too thick. The journey to a happier, mentally-healthy you starts with one step, one thought, and one page turned in this book. Let's explore together.

2.8 Thriving Mindset

As we wind down this chapter, I want to discuss about something super special: crafting a thriving mindset. It's like building your very own mental toolbox, filled with shiny tools that help you navigate every twist and turn life throws at you. Think of it as your secret superpower in this grand adventure called retirement.

So, what's the magic potion for a thriving mindset? Well, it's a mix!

1. Embrace Change: Remember when bell-bottoms were all the rage, and then suddenly, they weren't? Just like fashion, life's trends keep changing. Being open to change keeps you in vogue in the ever-evolving show of life.

2. Stay Curious: Hey, did you know otters hold hands when they sleep so they don't drift away? Fascinating, right? Keeping that spark of curiosity alive makes everyday a school day, but with more fun and fewer exams.

3. Celebrate Wins, Big or Small: Whether it's finally mastering a new recipe or just getting out of bed on a lazy day – each victory counts. And between you and me, I think retirement is full of 'em.

4. Cultivate Gratitude: When in doubt, count your blessings! It might sound cliché, but trust me, focusing on the silver linings turns regular days into extraordinary ones.

5. Be Your Own Cheerleader: Some days, the pep talks need to come from within. So, stand tall in front of that mirror and remind yourself, "I've got this!" Spoiler alert: You totally do.

Now, while having a toolkit is fantastic, remember to use those tools. Dive into the activities in this book, have hearty chats with loved ones, or simply soak in a sunset. Life's this vast, colorful canvas, and with the right mindset, you can paint a masterpiece every day.

Remember, dear reader, your mindset isn't fixed. It's malleable, adaptable, and most importantly, trainable. As we journey through this book, let's pledge to feed our minds with positivity and nurture a thriving mindset that celebrates every moment of retirement. Onwards to brighter, better days!

CHAPTER 2 ACTIVITY CHECKLIST

Retirement Psychology

Purpose: This checklist will guide you in understanding and embracing the psychological aspects of retirement, helping you to foster a positive and proactive mindset as you transition.

Getting Started:

✓ **Self-Reflection:** Journal about your feelings and concerns related to retirement.

✓ **Share Stories:** Talk to a retired friend or family member about their experiences.

✓ **Set Expectations:** Identify what you hope to gain from your retirement.

Emotions & Feelings:

✓ **Emotional Audit:** Recognize and label the emotions you're experiencing.

✓ **Positive Perspective:** List three things you're excited about in retirement.

✓ **Overcoming Uncertainty:** Identify one fear or concern and discuss it with someone.

Identity & Worth:

✓ **Role Realization:** Think about the roles you play in life and how they might change.

✓ **Skills Showcase:** List the skills and attributes you bring to any new endeavor.

✓ **New Narratives:** Write a brief statement about your post-retirement identity.

Purpose & Meaning:

✓ **Passion Project:** Identify a project or hobby you've always wanted to pursue.

✓ **Legacy Letter:** Write a letter to a younger family member sharing life lessons.

✓ **Day in Life:** Design your ideal retirement day.

Social Ties & Relationships:

✓ **Social Survey:** Assess your current social connections and desired future ones.

✓ **New Networks:** Join a community or interest group.

✓ **Bridge Building:** Strengthen relationships you wish to maintain in retirement.

Reflective Corner:

1. **Growth Glimpse:** How have your views on retirement evolved since starting this chapter?

2. **Forward Focus:** What's one new activity or routine you want to introduce?

Bonus Action:

✓ **Book Boost:** Pick up a self-help or psychology book to further explore retirement mindset.

Note: The transition to retirement is a journey of personal growth. Remember to be patient with yourself and revisit this checklist as needed to ensure a smooth emotional and psychological transition.

Chapter 3:
Active Living-Physical Activities

"Getting fit: Because round is not the preferred shape."

Chapter 3: Active Living - Physical Activities

3.1 Exercise for a Strong Body

Hey there, fitness enthusiast!

Diving right into the world of active living, let's kick things off by giving our hearts a bit of an adrenaline rush. You know, the thing that goes "thump-thump" inside your chest? Let's keep it happy, healthy, and hopping to a lively beat.

Cardiovascular Activities: Keeping That Heartbeat Groovy

When people talk about cardio, it's not about that dreadful memory of running laps in school (unless you were the sporty type who loved it). Nope. It's about finding joy in activities that make your heart feel alive and young!

1. Walk the World: Start simple. Walking might sound mundane, but it's a gentle way to get your heart rate up. Think of it as a chat between your feet and the earth, each step sharing a story.

2. Heart-thumping Running: Feel the rhythm of your feet, the wind against your face, and the world passing by. Whether it's a park, a treadmill, or a city street, running offers a quick cardio boost.

3. Dive into Aerobics: Remember those 80s aerobics videos? Well, aerobics is still alive and kicking. Get into the groove with some upbeat music and move those limbs.

4. Jump It Out: Skipping isn't just for kids on the playground. Grab a jump rope and hop to the beat. It's fun, and oh boy, your heart will love you for it!

5. Get those Steps In: Invest in a simple pedometer or a smartwatch and challenge yourself daily. Can you reach 10,000 steps today?

The beauty of cardiovascular exercises is that they can be as laid-back or as intense as you want them to be. And the best part? Every beat, step, and jump is a thank-you note to your heart for all its hard work.

In the next segment, we'll explore how you can go beyond just cardio and build strength. But for now, let that heart play its happy tunes!

Strength Training: Becoming Your Own Superhero

Alright, now that our hearts are humming a happy tune, let's talk muscles! No, you don't need to aspire to look like the next Marvel superhero (though that'd be cool), but a little strength training can make daily tasks easier and keep your body in top shape.

What is Strength Training, Really?

Strength training isn't just about lifting heavy weights in a gym surrounded by big biceps and grunting noises. It's about challenging your muscles, big or small, to handle resistance and come out stronger on the other side.

1. Start with the Basics – Bodyweight Exercises:

- ✓ **Push-ups:** Not just for army recruits! They're great for strengthening the chest and shoulders. And don't stress if you can't do a full one yet; starting on your knees is absolutely fine.

- ✓ **Squats:** Think of it as sitting on an invisible chair and then standing up. It's that simple. Plus, your legs and butt will thank you.

- ✓ **Lunges:** Walking or stationary, lunges are like a little love letter to your leg muscles.

2. Resistance Bands – Stretchy but Mighty: Before hitting the weights, these bands can be your best friends. They're portable, versatile, and oh-so-effective. Try bicep curls or leg lifts with these to feel the burn.

3. Dumbbells – Small Weights, Big Impact: You don't need to go heavy. Start with a weight that feels challenging but doable. Bicep curls, shoulder presses, and even squats can be enhanced with these little powerhouses.

4. Machines & More: If you feel like diving deeper, gyms offer various machines targeted at specific muscle groups. Always ask a trainer to show you the ropes first.

5. Remember to Rest: Muscles grow and repair when they rest, not when they're working. So, ensure you're giving yourself recovery days.

The best part of strength training? That awesome feeling when you carry all the grocery bags in one trip without breaking a sweat. It's the little victories that count!

In the next segment, we'll focus on the dance of flexibility and balance. It's not just about power; it's also about grace and movement. Stay tuned and stay strong!

Flexibility and Balance Exercises: The Graceful Dance of Aging

After flexing those muscles with strength training, it's time to introduce them to flexibility and balance exercises. Think of these activities as the harmonizing background vocals to the main tune of our body's song. They bring fluidity, poise, and help us avoid those unexpected trips and slips.

Stretching it Out: Why Flexibility Matters

Being flexible isn't just about impressing friends with feats like touching your toes. It's about keeping your muscles long, limber, and ready for any movement life throws at you.

Good Ol' Stretching:

✓ **Forward Bends:** These are perfect for the hamstrings and the lower back. It's like each tension point melts away.

✓ **Arm and Shoulder Stretches:** This helps release tension, especially if you've been lifting or carrying things around.

✓ **Quad Stretch:** For this, hold onto a chair and grab one ankle behind you. It feels like giving your leg a gentle stretch.

Yoga – The Ancient Art of Stretching & Relaxing: From the downward dog to the warrior pose, yoga offers a plethora of poses that help with both flexibility and relaxation. And it's more about the journey than trying to perfect each pose.

Pilates – Core and More: Think of Pilates as yoga's modern counterpart. It focuses on core strength and flexibility, giving your body's center stage a chance to shine.

Balancing Act: Staying Steady as You Go

Balance is crucial for daily activities and preventing falls.

Tai Chi – Slow and Steady: This ancient Chinese art form is like meditation in motion. It comprises gentle, flowing movements that center and stabilize you.

Stand on One Foot: It sounds simple, but it's effective. Just hold onto a sturdy surface, lift one foot, and challenge yourself to hold the position.

Balance Walk: Walk heel to toe as if you're on an imaginary tightrope. It's excellent for coordination!

Fitness Balls: Sitting on one of these engages the core muscles and challenges your balance. It's a fun and effective tool for your exercise routine.

Dancing: Whether it's a waltz, tango, or just grooving to your favorite tunes, dancing is wonderful for balance and for lifting spirits.

As we continue our journey into active living, remember it's not about achieving perfection. It's about progress, enjoying every step, and embracing each stretch and balance pose along the way.

Up next, we're headed outdoors to embrace the beauty of nature while keeping active. Ready for some fresh air and adventure?

3.2 Outdoor Adventures: Embracing the World Outside

Hiking and Nature Walks: A Step into the Wild

There's something profoundly therapeutic about stepping onto a trail, with the scent of earth and the sound of birds surrounding you. It's an invitation to both adventure and introspection. So, lace up those hiking boots and let's take a stroll into the world of hiking and nature walks.

The Lure of the Trail

Hiking isn't just about the destination; it's about the journey. Whether you're heading up a challenging mountain trail or a gentle path in the park, every step is a dance with nature.

Types of Trails:

✓ **Beginner Trails:** These are often flat, well-maintained, and offer plenty of resting spots. Perfect for those who want a relaxed stroll with nature.

✓ **Intermediate Trails:** A bit of challenge, some elevation changes, but still very doable. Remember to pack some water and snacks!

✓ **Advanced Trails:** For the more seasoned hikers, these trails often involve steeper climbs and require a bit more stamina.

Equipment and Prep: While nature is inviting, it pays to be prepared.

✓ **Good Hiking Shoes:** Your feet will thank you!

✓ **Weather-appropriate Clothing:** Layer up or down depending on the forecast.

✓ **Water and Snacks:** Stay hydrated and energized.

✓ **Navigation Tools:** A map or a hiking app can guide your way.

The Benefits of a Nature Walk

You don't have to climb a mountain to enjoy the benefits of the great outdoors. A simple walk in your local park or nature reserve can:

✓ **Boost Your Mood:** Nature has a way of melting away stress.

✓ **Improve Physical Health:** Walking is an excellent low-impact exercise.

✓ **Connect with Nature:** Spotting birds, trees, and maybe even some wildlife!

✓ **Walking Clubs:** Join a local walking or hiking group! It's a fantastic way to meet people, share experiences, and explore new trails together.

Safety First

Always let someone know where you're going, stick to the paths, and carry a basic first aid kit.

In essence, hiking and nature walks offer an opportunity to connect — with nature, with others, and most importantly, with ourselves. As we delve deeper into our outdoor adventures, keep an open heart to the lessons nature teaches us and the wonders that every trail unfolds.

Stay tuned, because up next, we're going to pedal our way through another fantastic outdoor activity. Can you guess what it is?

Biking and Cycling: Pedal Your Way to Adventure

Ah, the humble bicycle! Not only is it an eco-friendly mode of transport, but it's also a passport to adventures both big and small. Whether you're zipping down city lanes or exploring countryside trails, biking offers a unique blend of exhilaration and relaxation.

The Joy of Two Wheels

When you hop on a bike, it's like tapping into a forgotten piece of childhood. The thrill of the wind against your face, the world rushing by — it's freedom on two wheels.

Types of Biking:

✓ **Road Biking:** Racing down paved roads, feeling every curve and straight stretch. It's all about speed and endurance.

✓ **Mountain Biking:** This is where things get rugged. Tackling dirt trails, rocky paths, and challenging terrains.

✓ **Recreational Cycling:** Casual rides through the park or around your neighborhood. Perfect for a relaxing day out.

Gear Up

Just like with hiking, the right gear can make all the difference.

✓ **Helmet:** Safety first! A snug-fitting helmet can be a lifesaver.

✓ **Proper Footwear:** Ditch the flip-flops; opt for sturdy shoes.

✓ **Water Bottle Holder:** Staying hydrated is key, especially on longer rides.

Benefits of Biking

Beyond the sheer joy of it, biking has some tangible perks:

✓ **Physical Fitness:** It's a great cardio workout and excellent for toning muscles.

✓ **Eco-Friendly:** Reduce your carbon footprint one pedal at a time.

✓ **Mental Well-being:** Just like a car, sometimes our minds need to shift gears. Cycling can help clear the clutter.

Join the Community

Many towns and cities have biking clubs or groups that host regular rides. It's a wonderful way to socialize and discover new routes.

Safety on the Road

Remember to follow traffic rules, use hand signals, and always be aware of your surroundings. A little caution goes a long way in ensuring a safe and enjoyable ride.

All in all, biking is a versatile activity, suitable for both adrenaline junkies and those looking for a tranquil escape. So, grab your bike, hit the road or trail, and let the adventure begin! And while we're on the topic of adventures, our next one might just get your fingers a little dirty. Any guesses?

Gardening and Horticulture: Cultivate a Green Sanctuary

Let's talk about plants, dirt, and the deep satisfaction that comes from nurturing life. Gardening isn't just about producing colorful blooms or harvesting fresh veggies. It's a therapeutic journey, a chance to reconnect with nature, and an opportunity to create something beautiful.

Why Garden? There's a certain magic in planting a seed, tending to it, and watching it grow. It's like painting a picture, but instead of colors, you're using nature.

Types of Gardening:

✓ **Flower Gardening:** Brighten up your space with roses, tulips, sunflowers – you name it.

✓ **Vegetable Gardening:** Fresh tomatoes, crunchy carrots, and zesty herbs, right from your backyard.

✓ **Container Gardening:** Limited space? No problem. Pots and planters can bring life to even the tiniest of balconies.

Tools of the Trade

Getting your hands dirty is half the fun, but a few tools can make the process smoother:

✓ **Gloves:** Protect your hands from cuts and dirt.

✓ **Trowel:** Your trusty partner for planting.

✓ **Watering Can:** Keep those plants hydrated!

Benefits of Gardening

It's not just the plants that bloom:

✓ **Physical Health:** Digging, planting, weeding – it's a workout in disguise.

✓ **Mental Relaxation:** Many people find gardening to be a form of meditation.

✓ **Fresh Produce:** If you opt for veggies and herbs, the taste of home-grown food is unbeatable.

Join a Garden Club

Discover the joys of communal gardening, share tips, and maybe swap some plants. Being part of a community can make the experience even more enriching.

Tips for Beginners:

✓ **Start Small:** It can be tempting to turn your whole yard into a garden, but it's best to start with a small patch or a few containers.

✓ **Research:** Some plants need more sun; others thrive in the shade. Know what you're planting.

✓ **Patience:** Plants take time. Don't get disheartened if your garden doesn't look magazine-ready in the first month.

In the end, gardening is about enjoying the process as much as the results. Whether you're looking for a peaceful retreat, a hobby, or just some fresh air, the garden is where life blossoms. And speaking of outdoor activities, our next segment takes you on even more thrilling adventures. Ready to continue the journey?

CHAPTER 3 ACTIVITY CHECKLIST

Active Living - Physical Activities

Purpose: This checklist aims to guide you towards adopting a diverse range of physical activities, promoting overall well-being and embracing nature.

Exercise for a Strong Body:

- Cardiovascular Activities:
✓ Set a weekly cardio goal: __ minutes of walking/jogging/cycling.
✓ Explore a new cardio class or online video.
- Strength Training:
✓ Try a beginner weightlifting or resistance band routine.
✓ Designate specific days for upper body, lower body, and core workouts.
- Flexibility and Balance Exercises:
✓ Incorporate daily stretching into your routine.
✓ Try a basic yoga or tai chi sequence focusing on balance.

Outdoor Adventures:

- **Hiking and Nature Walks:**
✓ Plan a bi-weekly hike or nature walk.
✓ Discover a new trail or park in your vicinity.
- **Biking and Cycling:**
✓ Schedule a monthly recreational bike ride.
✓ Explore a cycling trail or path you haven't tried before.
- **Gardening and Horticulture:**
✓ Dedicate an hour each week to gardening.
✓ Start a new plant project: flower, vegetable, or herb.

Reflective Corner:

1. **Personal Best:** Note down a recent achievement in your active living journey.
2. **Roadblocks:** Identify challenges you're facing and think of a way to navigate them.

Bonus Action:

✓ **Wellness Connect:** Consider reaching out to a fitness expert or joining a group class to diversify your regimen.

Note: Everyone's journey in active living is unique. Adjust these activities based on your needs and capabilities. Remember to enjoy the process!

Chapter 4:
Expressing Creativity -
Art and DIY

"Getting crafty might involve more
wine than originally planned."

Chapter 4: Expressing Creativity - Art and DIY

Welcome to the World of Creation!

Every one of us has a spark of creativity inside, sometimes it just needs a nudge to come alive. Whether it's the allure of a blank canvas, the charm of fresh clay, or the vision of a DIY project, there's a world of potential in our hands. This chapter is all about discovering that inner artist and letting them play, experiment, and create. So, let's roll up our sleeves and paint our world with the colors of imagination!

4.1 Artistic Endeavors

Painting and Drawing

Ah, the joy of picking up a brush or a pencil and letting it dance across paper! Painting and drawing have been humankind's favorite ways of expressing thoughts, dreams, and emotions for ages.

1. **Why It's So Cool:**

✓ **Immediate Gratification:** See your thoughts come alive in color and form right before your eyes. Every stroke tells a part of your story.

✓ **Versatility:** From watercolors to charcoal, there are various mediums you can experiment with.

✓ **A Path to Mindfulness:** Believe it or not, the act of drawing or painting can be meditative. It grounds you in the moment, allowing you to focus on each line and shade.

2. **Getting Started:**

✓ **Materials:** Begin with basic sketching pencils, a few brushes, and paints. Don't forget a good quality art pad!

✓ **Classes:** Look for local art classes or online tutorials. They can provide structure as you begin.

✓ **Practice Makes Perfect:** The more you draw or paint, the better you'll get. So, keep at it!

3.   **Inspiration Everywhere:**

✓ **Nature:** Step outside! From a blooming flower to a tranquil lakeside, nature is brimming with scenes waiting to be captured.

✓ **Photos:** Use family photos or travel pictures as references.

✓ **Feelings:** Had a dreamy day or a gloomy afternoon? Express it on canvas. Your emotions can guide your color palette and strokes.

Remember, there's no right or wrong in art. It's all about expressing yourself. So, even if your first few sketches resemble abstract art more than the intended portrait, don't get disheartened. Every great artist started with simple doodles!

Writing and Journaling

Words, much like colors and strokes, have their magic. They can craft worlds, conjure emotions, and capture moments that a photograph might miss. Let's dive into the realm of writing and journaling, shall we?

1.   **The Magic of Words:**

✓ **Preserving Memories:** Ever had a day you wished you could bottle up and keep? Writing does that. It's a snapshot of your thoughts, capturing moments in intricate detail.

✓ **Therapeutic Value:** Pouring out feelings onto paper can be cathartic. It helps process emotions and makes sense of whirlwind days.

✓ **Creativity Unleashed:** From fantasy tales to poetic musings, the sky's the limit. Your imagination gets wings with words.

2.   **Finding Your Writing Niche:**

✓ **Journals:** Think of it as a dialogue with yourself. Chronicle your days, dreams, hopes, and even the random thoughts that flit through your mind.

✓ **Short Stories or Poetry:** Let your imagination run wild. Create characters, spin tales, or capture emotions in verse.

✓ **Blogging:** Share your experiences, insights, or expertise with the world. The internet can be your global audience!

3.   **Starting Points:**

✓ **Prompt Books:** These are filled with ideas to kickstart your writing journey.

✓ **Old Photos:** They can bring a flood of memories, perfect to pen down.

✓ **Observations:** The world around you, the coffee shop's bustle, or the park's tranquility, can be your muse.

4.   **Tips to Keep the Flow:**

✓ **Consistency:** Make it a habit. Write a little every day, even if it's just a line or two.

✓ **No Pressure:** It's okay if not every day's entry is profound or poetic. Some days, a grocery list is poetic enough!

✓ **Join Writing Groups:** These communities can offer feedback, support, and motivation.

Writing and journaling are about finding your voice and reveling in the joy of expression. So, grab that pen, open up that notebook, and let's begin this beautiful journey of words!

Music and Instrument Playing

Ah, the melodious world of music! It's said that where words fail, music speaks. And isn't that the truth? Whether you've always been a fan or you're just beginning to explore this realm, playing an instrument or simply immersing yourself in tunes can be incredibly fulfilling. Let's strum our way through this, shall we?

1.   **The Universal Language of Music:**

✓ **Emotion Amplifier:** Ever noticed how a particular song can uplift your spirits or make you nostalgic? That's the power of music. It resonates with our souls.

✓ **Brain Booster:** Learning an instrument is not just fun, it's brain exercise! It sharpens memory and enhances cognitive skills.

✓ **Social Connect:** Playing music, whether solo or in a group, can be a wonderful way to bond with others.

2.   **Choosing Your Instrument:**

✓ **Strings:** From the soft melodies of a guitar to the deep tones of a cello, string instruments have a vast range.

✓ **Wind:** Flutes, saxophones, clarinets – they can produce some of the most hauntingly beautiful notes.

✓ **Percussion:** If rhythm is your thing, drums, bongos, or even tambourines might be your calling.

3.   **Taking the First Step:**

✓ **Online Lessons:** Thanks to the internet, masterclasses are just a click away.

✓ **Local Music Schools:** Many local communities offer beginner courses. Plus, it's a great way to meet fellow enthusiasts.

✓ **Self-Learning:** With determination, a good instrument, and perhaps some instructional books, you can embark on a self-guided journey.

4.   **Tips to Stay in Tune:**

✓ **Practice Regularly:** Just like any skill, consistency is key in music.

✓ **Enjoy the Journey:** Don't get disheartened by initial hiccups. Remember, every maestro was once a beginner.

✓ **Share Your Music:** Play for friends, family, or even start a small YouTube channel. Sharing can be both fun and motivational.

Music is not just about playing notes; it's about playing with emotions. So, whether you pick up a harmonica or sit down at a grand piano, let your heart sing along!

4.2 DIY Projects

Rolling up your sleeves and diving into a hands-on project can be one of the most satisfying feelings. It's about taking control, crafting with love, and watching your vision come to life. In this chapter, we explore the world of DIY, where every creation tells a story of passion and persistence. Let's start with our homes, the cozy corners we cherish.

Home Improvement

Our homes are our sanctuaries. Every corner and every space tells a tale, and there's always room for a new chapter. Making improvements, even the little ones, can add a fresh spark and breathe life into familiar surroundings. Ready to don those DIY hats? Let's get to it!

1. **The Beauty of Beginnings:**

✓ **Why DIY?:** It's personal, cost-effective, and gives a sense of accomplishment. Plus, it's downright fun!

✓ **Starting Small:** If you're new, consider beginning with minor changes or upgrades. This could be painting a wall, changing handles, or introducing a new shelf.

2. **Areas to Explore:**

✓ **Painting and Wallpapering:** A change in wall color or a chic wallpaper can offer a room a completely new feel.

✓ **Furniture Makeovers:** Don't toss that old chair! A fresh coat of paint or new upholstery can make wonders.

✓ **Space Utilization:** Create extra storage under the stairs or design that unused corner into a cozy reading spot.

3. **Safety First:**

✓ **Tools and Gear:** It's essential to have the right tools for the job. Always remember safety first—goggles and gloves are must-haves!

✓ **Know Your Limits:** DIY is empowering, but for complex tasks, especially those related to electricity or plumbing, it's wise to call in the professionals.

4. **Finishing Touches:**

✓ **Decor and Accessories:** Once the major tasks are behind you, it's time to sprinkle some magic. Choose decor pieces that resonate with you.

✓ **Landscaping:** If you have an outdoor space, a few changes can make it even more inviting. Consider new plants or outdoor furniture.

With every nail driven and every brushstroke, you're making your living space more 'you'. Ready to give your home that special touch?

Crafting and Handmade Creations

Crafting is like sprinkling a little bit of your soul onto a blank piece of material. It's where imagination takes the front seat, and magic happens. With every stitch, cut, and glue, you're pouring your personality, emotions, and creativity. From gifts for loved ones to unique art pieces for your living space, let's dive into the beautiful world of crafting and handmade creations.

1.   **Getting Started:**

✓ **Choosing Your Craft:** From sewing to beadwork, from paper mache to clay modeling, there's a world of crafts waiting for you.

✓ **Essential Supplies:** Depending on your craft, you'll need some basic supplies. Most local craft stores or online shops can set you up with a starter kit.

✓ **Crafting Space:** Create a designated space for crafting—even a small table can be your creative corner. It helps to keep all your supplies organized and inspires you to dive in.

2.   **Popular Crafting Ideas:**

✓ **Paper Crafts:** Greeting cards, scrapbooking, origami, and quilling are beautiful ways to start.

✓ **Fabric and Thread:** Think of embroidery, quilting, or even making your own clothes or accessories.

✓ **Jewelry Making:** Design your own necklaces, bracelets, or earrings. The combinations are endless!

✓ **Upcycling:** Turn old, unused items into something new and beautiful. That old glass jar? Now it's a vintage candle holder.

3.   **Crafting for Wellness:**

✓ **Mindfulness and Focus:** Crafting often requires concentration, helping you stay present and engaged.

✓ **Therapeutic Benefits:** Many find crafting to be a form of therapy, helping to alleviate stress and boost mood.

✓ **Social Connections:** Join crafting groups or workshops. Share your creations online. The crafting community is vast and supportive.

4.   **Sharing Your Creations:**

✓ **Gifts With a Personal Touch:** Handmade crafts make heartfelt gifts. Every creation tells a story, and who wouldn't want a present made with love?

✓ **Selling Your Crafts:** Consider setting up a stall at local craft fairs or selling online through platforms like Etsy.

✓ **Workshops and Classes:** Once you've honed your skills, consider teaching others. It's a wonderful way to share the joy of crafting.

Crafting isn't just about creating beautiful things; it's a journey of self-discovery and expression. So grab those supplies and let your creativity flow!

Woodworking and Carpentry

Ah, the allure of wood! There's something genuinely magical about turning a simple piece of timber into a functional or decorative item. It's a dance between man, tool, and material. From the fresh scent of sawdust to the satisfaction of a finished project, woodworking and carpentry can be both a fulfilling hobby and a practical skill. Ready to dive in? Let's explore!

1.   **The Basics:**

✓ **Understanding the Wood:** Just like every paint has its canvas, every woodworking project has its wood. Learn about the different types of wood and their best uses.

✓ **Tools of the Trade:** Whether it's a simple hand saw or a power drill, knowing your tools is the first step. Remember, safety first!

✓ **Your Workspace:** A sturdy workbench, good lighting, and organized tools make all the difference. Even a corner of your garage can become a carpentry haven.

2.   **Starting Projects for Beginners:**

✓ **Simple Boxes:** Great for storage or as gifts. Mastering a basic box teaches you about measurements and joining techniques.

✓ **Shelves:** Functional and easy to customize. Plus, who doesn't need more shelf space?

✓ **Stools or Benches:** These offer a little more challenge but are incredibly rewarding once finished.

3. **Woodworking for Wellness:**

✓ **Physical Exercise:** It's not just about the brain; woodworking can be a good workout, especially when using hand tools.

✓ **Mental Clarity:** Focusing on precise cuts and measurements keeps your mind sharp and clear.

✓ **Tangible Results:** There's undeniable satisfaction in seeing, touching, and using something you've crafted from scratch.

4. **Deepening Your Skills:**

✓ **Join a Class or Workshop:** Learn from seasoned carpenters, share experiences, and perhaps even make some woodworking buddies.

✓ **Tackle Bigger Projects:** As your confidence grows, consider more complex projects like cabinets, tables, or even small pieces of furniture.

✓ **Restoration:** Breathe life into old or damaged wooden items. It's eco-friendly and gives objects a second chance.

5. **Sharing and Celebrating:**

✓ **Gift Your Creations:** A handcrafted wooden item makes a special, lasting gift.

✓ **Start a Blog or YouTube Channel:** Document your woodworking journey and share tips and tricks with fellow enthusiasts.

✓ **Sell Your Crafts:** From local craft fairs to online platforms, there's an audience eager for handcrafted wooden items.

Whether it's the rhythmic sound of chiseling, the spin of the lathe, or the hum of a saw, woodworking is a melody of creation. So, roll up those sleeves and let the wood inspire you!

CHAPTER 4 ACTIVITY CHECKLIST

Expressing Creativity - Art and DIY

Purpose: This checklist seeks to inspire you to channel your inner artist and craftsperson, allowing self-expression to shine through various mediums.

Artistic Endeavors:

- **Painting and Drawing:**
  ✓ Create a simple sketch or painting once a week.
  ✓ Explore a new painting or drawing technique or medium.
- **Writing and Journaling:**
  ✓ Dedicate a time each day for journaling or creative writing.
  ✓ Share a story or poem with a friend or family member.
- **Music and Instrument Playing:**
  ✓ Practice or learn a new song or piece.
  ✓ Explore a new musical genre or instrument.

DIY Projects:

- **Home Improvement:**
  ✓ Choose a small area of your home to revamp or redecorate.
  ✓ Learn a new home repair or improvement skill.
- **Crafting and Handmade Creations:**
  ✓ Start a new craft project: knitting, crocheting, or beading.
  ✓ Attend a craft workshop or watch an online tutorial.
- **Woodworking and Carpentry:**
  ✓ Design a simple woodworking project, e.g., a birdhouse or shelf.
  ✓ Gather or purchase necessary tools and materials.

Reflective Corner:

1. **Joyful Moments:** Jot down a recent creation that brought you immense joy.
2. **Creative Challenges:** Pinpoint any obstacles in your creative process and brainstorm solutions.

Bonus Action:

✓ **Art Connect:** Consider visiting an art exhibition or joining a local art group to expand your horizons.

Note: Remember, creativity isn't about perfection. It's about expression, exploration, and most importantly, fun!

Chapter 5:
Forever Learning –
Lifelong Education

"Learning: Because you can teach an
old dog new tricks!"

Chapter 5: Forever Learning - Lifelong Education

Remember when we were kids, and every day seemed to bring a new discovery? Whether it was a new word, a fascinating bug in the yard, or the sheer joy of a storybook, learning was a magical experience. The good news? That magic doesn't have to end just because we've added a few more candles to our birthday cake. In this digital age, opportunities for learning are abundant, accessible, and often free. This chapter is a tribute to the lifelong learner in each of us, showcasing the myriad of ways we can feed our ever-curious minds.

5.1 Continuous Education

Online Courses and E-Learning

Ah, the wonders of the internet! Gone are the days when learning a new skill meant traveling to a brick-and-mortar institution or shelling out big bucks for an evening class. Today, from the comfort of our homes, we can dive deep into nearly any subject, thanks to online courses and e-learning platforms. Let's unpack this a bit:

1.   **Diverse Range of Topics:**

✓ **From A to Z:** Whether you want to explore astrophysics or zero in on Zen meditation, there's a course out there for you.

✓ **Skill Building:** Always wanted to code? Or perhaps try your hand at digital art? The online realm is your oyster.

✓ **Academic Courses:** Many renowned universities offer their courses online, either free or at a fraction of the cost.

2.   **Flexible Learning:**

✓ **Learn at Your Pace:** Got 15 minutes during lunch or an hour before bedtime? Use that time to learn.

✓ **Pause and Rewind:** Didn't catch something the first time? No worries. Review the material as often as you need.

✓ **Choose Your Environment:** Your favorite armchair, a sunny spot in the park, or a cozy cafe — learning can happen anywhere.

3.   **Interactive and Engaging:**

✓ **Video Lectures:** Often accompanied by visuals, making the content more digestible and fun.

✓ **Quizzes and Assignments:** Test your knowledge, get feedback, and track your progress.

✓ **Discussion Forums:** Engage with fellow learners, ask questions, and share insights.

4.   **Building a Learning Habit:**

✓ **Set Clear Goals:** Whether it's completing a course in a month or studying for 30 minutes daily, having a goal keeps you motivated.

✓ **Create a Study Space:** A dedicated space, however small, signals your brain that it's "learning time".

✓ **Celebrate Milestones:** Finished a module? Mastered a tricky concept? Give yourself a pat on the back!

5.   **Expanding Opportunities:**

✓ **Certificates and Diplomas:** Many platforms offer certifications upon completion, which can be a great addition to your resume.

✓ **Networking:** Connect with instructors and peers, opening doors to potential collaborations or career opportunities.

In a world that's rapidly evolving, staying updated and continuously learning isn't just a hobby—it's a necessity. And with e-learning, it's also a delight!

Workshops and Seminars

You know what's awesome about being human? That tingling sensation we get when we're in a room full of people, all eager to learn something new. Workshops and seminars provide just that—a collective energy, hands-on experiences, and the opportunity to rub elbows with experts and like-minded folks.

Let's dive into why these offline experiences are a fantastic complement to your online explorations:

1.   **Hands-On Learning:**

✓ **Practical Experience:** Unlike online courses where you're often a passive observer, workshops involve doing. Whether it's pottery, photography, or coding, you get to practice in real-time.

✓ **Immediate Feedback:** Made a mistake? Not sure if you're doing it right? Experts are right there to guide you on the spot.

2. **Networking Opportunities:**

✓ **Meet Like-Minded Individuals:** Sharing a learning experience often leads to lasting friendships or professional relationships.

✓ **Connect with Experts:** It's not every day you get to ask questions directly to an industry professional or a subject matter expert. Make the most of it!

3. **Deep Dives:**

✓ **Focused Sessions:** Workshops and seminars often tackle a specific topic in-depth, giving you a comprehensive understanding in a short time.

✓ **Interactive Discussions:** Engage in group debates, brainstorming sessions, and problem-solving exercises that stimulate your thinking.

4. **A Change of Scenery:**

✓ **Break the Routine:** Attending a workshop can be a refreshing change from your daily routine, offering new sights and experiences.

✓ **Travel Opportunities:** If the seminar is in a different city or even country, it's a perfect excuse for a mini vacation!

5. **Tangible Outcomes:**

✓ **Certificates and Skills:** Many workshops provide certificates upon completion, and the skills you acquire can be immediately put to use.

✓ **Resources and Materials:** Often, you'll walk away with resource lists, materials, or tools to continue your learning journey.

6. **Staying Motivated:**

✓ **Accountability:** When you've invested time and perhaps money to attend, you're more likely to fully engage and follow through.

✓ **Shared Enthusiasm:** There's something infectious about a group's collective excitement and motivation. It pushes you to give your best.

So, the next time you hear about a workshop or seminar in your city—or even elsewhere—give it a thought. It might just be the perfect way to spend a weekend, learn something new, and meet some fantastic people along the way!

Language Learning and Cultural Studies

Ah, the beauty of languages! Imagine being able to chat with a local in Paris, haggle at a market in Marrakech, or understand the lyrics of that catchy K-pop song. And it's not just about the words; it's the window into a new world, a different way of thinking, and a wealth of history and culture.

Let's embark on this linguistic journey and explore why diving into language learning and cultural studies can be a fulfilling venture in retirement:

1. **Brain Gym:**

✓ **Cognitive Boost:** Learning a new language is a fantastic workout for your brain. It improves memory, enhances multitasking abilities, and even delays cognitive aging. A win-win, right?

✓ **New Neural Pathways:** Your brain creates fresh connections as you grapple with grammar, pronunciation, and vocabulary.

2. **Cultural Appreciation:**

✓ **Understanding Nuances:** When you learn a language, you don't just learn words. You uncover customs, traditions, and the history embedded within those words.

✓ **Broadened Horizons:** By studying a culture, you gain a deeper appreciation of its art, music, literature, and culinary delights.

3. **Travel Enhanced:**

✓ **Local Connections:** Speaking even a bit of the local tongue can open doors during your travels. Locals appreciate when you make the effort, and it can lead to more authentic experiences.

✓ **Deeper Exploration:** Beyond the tourist spots, language skills enable you to delve into lesser-known areas, making your travel tales unique.

4.   **Personal Growth:**

✓ **Boosted Confidence:** There's a certain pride in being able to introduce yourself or order a meal in a different language. It's an accomplishment, no matter how small.

✓ **Patience and Perseverance:** Language learning is a journey with ups and downs, but it teaches resilience. Every mispronounced word or misunderstood sentence is a stepping stone.

5.   **Social Perks:**

✓ **New Friendships:** Language classes and cultural study groups are great places to meet people with similar interests.

✓ **Cultural Events:** Your newfound knowledge can be a ticket to enjoy foreign films, book readings, cultural festivals, and more without feeling lost.

6.   **Practical Applications:**

✓ **New Hobbies:** Maybe you'll start writing poetry in Spanish or cooking Korean dishes. The world becomes your playground!

✓ **Volunteer Opportunities:** Use your language skills to assist in community outreach or even teach others.

The beautiful part? You don't need to aim for fluency. Every word learned, every phrase practiced brings joy and growth. Dive into the vast ocean of languages and cultures, and you'll find treasures aplenty.

5.2 Literary Pursuits

Book Clubs and Reading Groups

Remember those school days when you'd dive deep into a book, get lost in its world, and then impatiently wait for a friend to read it so you could talk about it for hours? Well, guess what? With book clubs and reading groups, you can relive that magic! 📚

Let's unravel why joining or even starting one can be an enriching experience:

1. **Shared Joy:**

✓ **Bond Over Books:** There's something special about discussing characters, plot twists, and even arguing over the ending of a book with fellow enthusiasts.

✓ **Relive Stories:** As you discuss, you'll revisit the story, often noticing details you missed the first time.

2. **Broaden Your Reading Horizons:**

✓ **Diverse Genres:** Being in a club often means reading books you might never have picked up on your own. From sci-fi to historical fiction, you'll be exposed to a wide array.

✓ **Author Discoveries:** Learn about new authors or international bestsellers you might have overlooked.

3. **Cognitive Benefits:**

✓ **Deeper Analysis:** Discussing a book can lead to a more profound understanding, as you see it from multiple perspectives.

✓ **Boosted Retention:** Talking about what you've read helps in retaining the information, be it fiction or non-fiction.

4. **Social Connections:**

✓ **Meet Like-minded Individuals:** Book clubs are a great way to make friends who share a love for literature.

✓ **Cultural Exchange:** Reading international literature and discussing it provides insight into various cultures and lifestyles.

5. **Personal Growth:**

✓ **Confidence in Expression:** Presenting your interpretation or viewpoint in a group setting can boost your confidence and communication skills.

✓ **Emotional Exploration:** Literature often taps into universal emotions. Discussing them can lead to self-awareness and emotional intelligence.

6. **Fun and Relaxation:**

✓ **Themed Gatherings:** Some clubs have themed meetings, like dressing up as characters or making dishes from the book's setting.

✓ **Local Author Sessions:** Some groups invite local authors for discussions, providing a unique perspective.

7. **Accessibility:**

✓ **Digital Age Benefits:** Can't find a local group or prefer staying in? There are countless online book clubs and groups you can join, making participation easier than ever.

Reading is a solitary activity, but when shared, it takes on a new dimension. Whether you're revisiting classics, exploring new releases, or diving into non-fiction, doing it as part of a group can amplify the joy and insights gained.

Creative Writing and Storytelling

Once upon a time, in the depths of your imagination, there's a story brewing. Whether it's an adventurous tale, a heartwarming narrative, or a gripping mystery, it's waiting to spill out onto paper. Let's explore why delving into creative writing and storytelling can be such a captivating journey:

1. **Personal Exploration:**

✓ **Deep Dive:** Writing often acts as a mirror, reflecting your thoughts, feelings, and experiences. It can be therapeutic, helping you understand yourself better.

✓ **Freedom of Expression:** With creative writing, there are no boundaries. Let your imagination run wild!

2. **Improving Cognitive Skills:**

✓ **Brain Exercise:** Crafting plots, developing characters, and setting scenes can stimulate your mind and keep it sharp.

✓ **Enhanced Vocabulary:** As you write more, you'll naturally pick up and incorporate new words, enriching your language.

3. **Emotional Outlet:**

✓ **Express and De-stress:** Putting emotions onto paper can be cathartic, acting as an outlet for feelings you might not express verbally.

✓ **Fiction as Therapy:** Creating a fictional world or characters can help process real-life events or emotions.

4. **Connecting with Others:**

✓ **Story Sharing:** Sharing your stories can connect you with readers, resonating with their experiences or sparking their imagination.

✓ **Writing Groups:** Joining writing groups or workshops can provide feedback, inspire new ideas, and create camaraderie among fellow writers.

5. **Legacy Building:**

✓ **Timeless Tales:** Your stories can be a legacy, leaving a part of you for future generations to discover and cherish.

✓ **Inspire Others:** Your writings might inspire someone else to start their journey, creating a ripple effect of storytellers.

6. **Skill Building:**

✓ **Craft Mastery:** The more you write, the better you get! It's a skill that evolves with practice.

✓ **Diverse Genres:** Experimenting with different genres, from poetry to short stories, can expand your skills and versatility.

7. **Enjoyment & Fulfillment:**

✓ **Pleasure of Creation:** There's a unique joy in creating something from scratch, and seeing a story take shape is deeply satisfying.

✓ **Pride in Publishing:** Whether you share your work on a blog, in a local magazine, or even publish a book, there's immense pride in seeing your work in print.

In essence, creative writing and storytelling aren't just about penning down tales. They are about exploring, understanding, and expressing oneself, all while enjoying the incredible journey of creation.

Literary Events and Author Talks

Ah, the bustling world of literary events and author talks! A realm where the pages of books come alive, and you get to be right there, soaking it all in. Whether you're a dedicated bookworm or just someone who enjoys a good conversation, these events offer treasures galore. Let's dive into why they're worth your time:

1. **Behind the Scenes:**

✓ **Author Insights:** Ever wonder why an author chose a particular twist or developed a character in a certain way? This is your chance to find out.

✓ **Creative Process:** Authors often share their journey of crafting a story, offering a sneak peek into their minds.

2. **Broaden Your Horizons:**

✓ **Diverse Voices:** Literary events showcase a variety of authors from different backgrounds, allowing you to explore diverse narratives and perspectives.

✓ **Genre Exploration:** Discover genres you might not usually gravitate towards. Who knows? You might find a new favorite.

3. **Community Building:**

✓ **Meeting Like-minded Folks:** Events are a wonderful place to connect with fellow book enthusiasts. Discussions over a plot twist are friendships in the making!

✓ **Engaging Debates:** Dive deep into discussions about themes, characters, and the world of literature as a whole.

4. **Inspiration & Motivation:**

✓ **Fuel Your Own Writing:** Listening to accomplished authors can spark your own creativity and drive to pen down your thoughts or stories.

✓ **Tips & Tricks:** Many authors offer advice on writing, publishing, and navigating the literary world.

5. **Personal Growth:**

✓ **Critical Thinking:** Engaging with complex narratives and themes can sharpen your analytical skills.

✓ **Empathy Building:** Exploring stories from different walks of life fosters understanding and compassion.

6. **Entertainment & Joy:**

✓ **Dynamic Readings:** There's something magical about hearing an author bring their words to life.

✓ **Interactive Sessions:** Many events have Q&A segments, allowing you to ask your burning questions or simply enjoy the banter.

7. **Supporting the Arts:**

✓ **Encouraging Authors:** Your presence at these events supports authors, motivating them to keep creating.

✓ **Promoting Literature:** By participating, you contribute to a thriving literary culture and community.

In a nutshell, literary events and author talks are a delightful blend of learning, entertainment, and community. They're not just about books; they're about experiences, connections, and the sheer joy of literature.

CHAPTER 5 ACTIVITY CHECKLIST

Forever Learning - Lifelong Education

Purpose: This checklist encourages you to continuously feed your curiosity, expand your horizons, and embrace the lifelong journey of learning.

Continuous Education:

- **Online Courses and E-Learning:**
  ✓ Explore an online platform and enroll in a course of interest.
  ✓ Complete a module or lesson each week.

- **Workshops and Seminars:**
  ✓ Research and attend a local or virtual workshop related to a passion or skill.
  ✓ Share your newly acquired knowledge with a friend.

- **Language Learning and Cultural Studies:**
  ✓ Choose a new language to learn; practice speaking or writing daily.
  ✓ Delve into the history or traditions of a specific culture.

Literary Pursuits:

- **Book Clubs and Reading Groups:**
  ✓ Join a local or online book club.
  ✓ Read the book of the month and participate in discussions.

- **Creative Writing and Storytelling:**
  ✓ Write a short story, poem, or personal essay.
  ✓ Share your piece in a writing group or with close friends.

- **Literary Events and Author Talks:**
  ✓ Attend a literary event, whether virtual or in-person.
  ✓ Engage in a Q&A with an author or submit a review.

Reflective Corner:

1. **Knowledge Nuggets:** Note a fascinating fact or piece of information you learned recently.
2. **Future Studies:** List down a subject or skill you're eager to dive into next.

Bonus Action:

✓ **Education Exchange:** Partner with a buddy and teach each other a new skill or topic.

Note: The world is a vast encyclopedia waiting for you to turn its pages. Stay curious!

Chapter 6:
Community Involvement

"Community involvement: because
Karma loves a helping hand!"

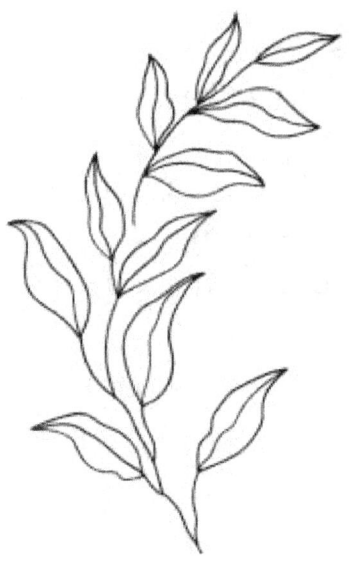

Chapter 6: Community Involvement

As we weave our way through the tapestry of life, it becomes clear that we're not just solitary figures moving on a vast canvas. We're part of a vibrant, interwoven community that shapes, influences, and is influenced by each of us. Engaging with this community, especially during retirement, not only fills our days with purpose but also connects us to the world in meaningful ways. This chapter focuses on how you can get involved and make a difference. After all, the spirit of community is all about giving, receiving, and growing together.

6.1 Volunteering & Giving Back

Community Service

We've all heard the saying, "It takes a village." Community service is the very embodiment of this sentiment. It's all about rolling up your sleeves, diving in, and helping to make that 'village' a better place for everyone. Here's why diving into community service is such a fabulous idea:

1. **Fulfillment & Joy:**

✓ **Making an Impact:** Even small acts can create ripples of change.

✓ **Personal Growth:** Serving others often leads to insights about oneself and the world around.

2. **Connections & Friendships:**

✓ **Meeting Diverse People:** Interacting with individuals from various backgrounds can be enlightening.

✓ **Shared Purpose:** Working towards a common goal fosters strong bonds.

3. **Learning & Skills:**

✓ **New Abilities:** From organizing events to manual tasks, community service can introduce you to new skills.

✓ **Problem Solving:** Facing and overcoming challenges in community projects can be a valuable experience.

4. **Health & Well-being:**

✓ **Physical Activity:** Many community service projects involve moving and working outdoors.

✓ **Mental Boost:** Helping others is proven to boost happiness and reduce stress.

5. **Local Understanding:**

✓ **Community Insights:** Engaging directly with local projects offers a deeper understanding of community needs and dynamics.

✓ **Cultural Appreciation:** Working with diverse groups can offer insights into different cultural practices and values.

6. **Legacy & Contribution:**

✓ **Making a Mark:** Your contributions can have long-lasting effects on the community.

✓ **Inspiring Others:** Your commitment can motivate others to join in and make a difference.

In essence, community service is a two-way street. While you offer your time, skills, and energy, you receive so much in return - from friendships and learning to a profound sense of fulfillment. It's a beautiful dance of give and take.

Nonprofit Organizations

The world is filled with passionate individuals and groups who are out there, day in and day out, trying to make a difference. Many of these champions find their home in nonprofit organizations. Whether it's battling climate change, promoting arts and culture, providing for the less fortunate, or countless other noble causes, nonprofits are the backbone of positive societal change. Here's how getting involved with them can enrich your retirement:

1. **Diverse Opportunities:**

✓ **Multiple Causes:** With countless nonprofits out there, you're sure to find one that aligns with your passion, be it animals, arts, education, or the environment.

✓ **Variety of Roles:** From administrative tasks to fieldwork, there's a plethora of roles to choose from.

2. **Purpose & Fulfillment:**

✓ **Making a Tangible Difference:** Nonprofits often work directly on the ground, ensuring your efforts have a visible impact.

✓ **Being Part of a Larger Mission:** There's something deeply rewarding about contributing to a cause bigger than oneself.

3. **Skill Development & Utilization:**

✓ **Applying Your Expertise:** Use your pre-retirement skills in meaningful ways, whether you were an accountant, teacher, or marketer.

✓ **Learning Anew:** Step out of your comfort zone and acquire new competencies, from digital skills to public speaking.

4. **Social Engagement & Networking:**

✓ **Meeting Like-Minded People:** Surround yourself with passionate individuals who share your zeal for change.

✓ **Building Lasting Bonds:** The camaraderie in nonprofits often leads to deep, lasting friendships.

5. **Understanding Global Perspectives:**

✓ **Diverse Interactions:** Many nonprofits operate globally, offering you a chance to interact with people from different parts of the world.

✓ **Grassroot Insights:** Understand global issues from the ground up, providing a more in-depth perspective.

6. **Legacy Building:**

✓ **Sustained Impact:** Your involvement can lead to projects and initiatives that continue to benefit society long after your direct involvement.

✓ **Mentorship:** Share your life experiences and skills with younger volunteers, guiding the next generation.

Remember, every bit counts. Whether you're helping out a few hours a week or diving into a full-time role, your contribution to nonprofit organizations can create waves of positive change, both for the world and for yourself.

Disaster Relief and Humanitarian Work

Let's talk about a different kind of adventure. One where the stakes are high, the challenges are real, and the rewards? They're beyond words. Disaster relief and humanitarian work is for those who feel a strong calling to help in situations where the need is greatest.

1. **Real-World Impact:**

✓ **Immediate Results:** When you provide food, water, or shelter to someone who's just lost everything, the gratitude you witness is instant and profound.

✓ **Saving Lives:** In many scenarios, the quick response of relief teams can mean the difference between life and death.

2. **Challenging Yet Rewarding:**

✓ **Test Your Limits:** This is not your typical volunteering. The conditions can be tough, and the work, relentless. But the sense of purpose? Unmatched.

✓ **Stories to Tell:** Each mission brings with it unforgettable stories of human resilience, hope, and the indomitable human spirit.

3. **Skill Utilization and Development:**

✓ **Specialized Roles:** Medics, logisticians, water and sanitation experts, and many others play crucial roles in disaster zones.

✓ **Learn on the Go:** Every mission is a lesson in adaptability, problem-solving, and teamwork.

4. **Deep Human Connections:**

✓ **Bonding Under Pressure:** Working side by side with others in intense situations creates lasting bonds of friendship and camaraderie.

✓ **Witnessing Resilience:** Seeing the strength of affected communities as they rebuild and heal is a humbling and transformative experience.

5. **Perspective Shift:**

✓ **Realizing the Essentials:** Such experiences make you appreciate the basics of life – clean water, food, shelter, and the love of family and community.

✓ **Valuing Time:** You'll learn to treasure moments of calm, joy, and the sheer beauty of human kindness in adversity.

6.   **How to Start:**

✓ **Training:** Organizations often provide necessary training for volunteers to equip them for the field.

✓ **Small Steps:** You don't have to jump into a war zone straight away. Start with local organizations, learn the ropes, and then decide how deep you want to dive.

For those with the heart and spirit for it, disaster relief and humanitarian work can be the most transformative journey of all. It's about rolling up your sleeves, diving in, and making a tangible difference when it matters most.

6.2 Mentorship & Sharing

Mentoring Youth and Adults

Imagine leaving a lasting impact on someone's life, lighting their path with the wisdom of your experiences. Mentoring is all about guiding, supporting, and enriching the lives of others, and it can be one of the most fulfilling roles you'll ever embrace in your life.

1. **Why Mentorship Matters:**

✓ **Passing the Torch:** Your life's lessons can become someone else's guiding light, helping them navigate through challenges and towards their dreams.

✓ **Two-Way Street:** While you guide your mentee, their fresh perspective and energy can rejuvenate and inspire you in return.

2. **Choosing Your Path:**

✓ **Youth Mentorship:** Connecting with young people can be invigorating. Share your experiences, listen to their dreams, and help them set strong foundations for their futures.

✓ **Adult Mentorship:** Adults too, often seek guidance at crossroads in their lives. Your expertise can help them transition careers, learn new skills, or simply find more meaning in their daily lives.

3. **Ways to Connect:**

✓ **Schools and Colleges:** Many educational institutions run mentorship programs. Dive in and help students in areas you're passionate about.

✓ **Professional Associations:** Offer your expertise to young professionals or peers looking for guidance in your industry or domain.

4. **Building Trust:**

✓ **Listen First:** Effective mentoring isn't just about giving advice. It's about listening, understanding, and then guiding.

✓ **Be Genuine:** Authenticity is key. Share both successes and mistakes, so your mentee gets a balanced view of reality.

5. **Celebrating Growth:**

✓ **Witnessing Progress:** One of the joys of mentoring is seeing your mentee grow, evolve, and achieve their goals.

✓ **Evolving Together:** As time goes on, the mentor-mentee relationship can evolve into one of mutual respect and friendship.

6. **Starting Your Mentorship Journey:**

✓ **Identify Your Strengths:** Understand where you can offer the most value.

✓ **Be Open-minded:** Every mentee is different. Approach each with an open heart and mind.

Mentorship is a dance of wisdom, respect, and mutual growth. When you invest time and heart in mentoring, you're not just shaping a life; you're building a legacy of knowledge and kindness.

Leading Workshops and Classes

So, you've lived, you've learned, and you've got a well of knowledge. Why not share it? Leading workshops or classes can be an excellent way to pass on what you've gathered over the years and, trust me, there's someone out there eager to learn from you.

1. **The Joy of Teaching:**

✓ **Sharing is Caring:** It's a gift to share what you've learned. And teaching, in many ways, is a form of giving back.

✓ **Revisiting and Refreshing:** When you teach, you often get the chance to revisit concepts and ideas, giving them new life.

2. **Choosing Your Topic:**

✓ **Your Passion:** Maybe it's painting, photography, cooking, or digital skills. Pick a subject you're passionate about.

✓ **Market Demand:** Research a bit to see what people are eager to learn these days. Maybe your unique skill is in high demand!

3. **Setting the Stage:**

✓ **Venue Selection:** You could host in community centers, local colleges, or even online platforms like Zoom or Skype.

✓ **Promotion:** Use social media, local newspapers, or community boards to let folks know about your classes.

4.   **Engaging Your Students:**

✓ **Interactive Sessions:** Encourage questions, debates, and discussions. Active learning always leaves a deeper impression.

✓ **Real-life Examples:** Share stories from your life or career that relate to the topic. It'll make the learning more relatable and memorable.

5.   **Feedback and Evolution:**

✓ **Seek Opinions:** After your session, ask for feedback. This can help you refine your teaching methods.

✓ **Continuous Learning:** The best teachers are also eager students. Stay updated with the latest in your domain to keep your sessions fresh.

6.   **The Ripple Effect:**

✓ **Inspire Change:** Even if just one person in your class takes away something valuable, imagine the ripple effect that can create in their life and the lives of those they touch.

✓ **Building a Community:** Over time, your workshops can lead to the formation of a community of like-minded individuals sharing, learning, and growing together.

When you stand in front of a group, eager to learn from your experiences, you realize that every challenge, every triumph, and every lesson of your life can illuminate someone else's path. So, go on, light up some lives!

Community Building Initiatives

Building a community isn't just about gathering people together. It's about creating connections, nurturing relationships, and fostering a sense of belonging. Think of it as helping weave a warm, cozy blanket that brings everyone in its fold closer.

1.   **Understanding Community Building:**

✓ **More than Just Numbers:** A community isn't just about how many people are in it, but how those people feel when they're part of it.

✓ **A Sense of Belonging:** At its core, a community gives everyone a feeling that they're in it together, cheering for each other's successes and supporting through the tough times.

2.   **Finding a Focus:**

✓ **Shared Interests:** Whether it's a hobby, a passion, or a cause, find that common thread that binds people together.

✓ **Local Needs:** Sometimes, community building is about addressing a local need or challenge. This could be a community garden, a neighborhood watch, or even a local book swap.

3.   **Organizing Events and Activities:**

✓ **Community Potlucks:** An age-old favorite, because who doesn't love food? Plus, it's a great way for neighbors to bond.

✓ **Workshops or Classes:** Like we discussed earlier, share a skill or invite others to do so.

✓ **Clean-up Drives:** Nothing like working together to beautify your local area.

4.   **Creating Safe Spaces:**

✓ **Open Dialogues:** Host sessions where people can voice concerns, discuss solutions, and share stories without judgment.

✓ **Celebrating Diversity:** Encourage cultural events or festivals that celebrate the different backgrounds of community members.

5.   **Using Technology:**

✓ **Online Platforms:** Websites or apps dedicated to your community can keep everyone updated on events, important dates, or local news.

✓ **Social Media Groups:** Platforms like Facebook or WhatsApp can be handy for quick communication among members.

6.   **Growing and Evolving:**

✓ **Feedback is Gold:** Regularly seek feedback on what the community loves and where they see room for improvement.

✓ **Stay Adaptable:** As the community grows, its needs may change. Be ready to adapt and evolve to keep the community spirit alive.

There's a simple joy in being part of something bigger than oneself. As you spearhead these community-building initiatives, you'll see the magic unfold – friendships blossoming, collaboration in action, and the heartwarming feeling of unity in diversity. Dive in, and let's build together!

CHAPTER 6 ACTIVITY CHECKLIST

Community Involvement

Purpose: Engage with the world around you, giving back and fostering connections that make a difference.

Volunteering & Giving Back:

- **Community Service:**

✓ Identify a local community project or event. Volunteer a few hours of your time.

✓ Reflect on the impact of your involvement.

- **Nonprofit Organizations:**

✓ Research a nonprofit organization whose mission resonates with you.

✓ Consider making a donation or offering your skills as a volunteer.

- **Disaster Relief and Humanitarian Work:**

✓ Explore opportunities with organizations that offer aid in crisis situations.

✓ Join a training program to prepare for participation in relief efforts.

Mentorship & Sharing:

- **Mentoring Youth and Adults:**

✓ Connect with a local school or community center to offer mentorship.

✓ Schedule regular check-ins with your mentee.

- **Leading Workshops and Classes:**

✓ Share your expertise by hosting a workshop or class.

✓ Gather feedback to refine and improve future sessions.

- **Community Building Initiatives:**

✓ Participate in or initiate a community project, like a neighborhood clean-up or tree planting.

✓ Engage neighbors or friends to join in.

Reflective Corner:

1. **Impact Moments:** Describe a moment during your community involvement that deeply touched you.

2. **Connection Chronicles:** Share a story about someone you met while volunteering or mentoring.

Bonus Action:

✓ **Community Chronicle:** Document your experiences through photos, videos, or journal entries. Share these memories with others or on social media to inspire more community involvement.

Note: Your actions, no matter how small, ripple through the community, creating waves of positive change.

Chapter 7:
Travel & Exploration

"Discovering new cultures, foods, and how to ask 'Where's the bathroom?' in ten languages!"

Chapter 7: Travel & Exploration

Ah, the allure of distant lands, the call of the unknown, the thrill of discovery! Travel is one of life's greatest adventures, a way to challenge ourselves, meet new people, and see the world from a fresh perspective. Whether you're exploring a neighboring town or venturing to a far-off continent, every journey enriches the soul. This chapter will be your passport to new horizons, guiding you on how to make the most of your travels, wherever the wind may take you.

7.1 New Horizons

Domestic Travel

Exploring one's own country can often be as fascinating as traveling abroad. Sometimes, the most breathtaking landscapes, rich histories, and heartwarming tales are waiting right at your doorstep.

1. **The Beauty of Home:**

✓ **Familiar Yet New:** Each state, region, or even town has its own distinct culture, history, and flavor. Rediscover your homeland.

✓ **Ease of Travel:** With no language barriers or visa requirements, domestic travel is often more spontaneous and stress-free.

2. **Destination Ideas:**

✓ **Historical Sites:** Take a trip down memory lane by visiting local monuments, museums, or heritage sites.

✓ **Natural Wonders:** Seek out national parks, beautiful lakes, or scenic routes close to home.

✓ **Festivals and Events:** Immerse yourself in local celebrations, fairs, or events to truly feel the heart of your nation.

3. **Planning Your Trip:**

✓ **Local Guides:** Consider hiring local guides to provide a deeper insight into the places you visit.

✓ **Travel Off-season:** This can often mean fewer crowds and better deals.

✓ **Staycations:** Even a weekend away in a neighboring town can refresh your mind.

4. **Getting Around:**

✓ **Road Trips:** Pack your bags, create a playlist, and hit the road. There's something magical about the journey itself.

✓ **Public Transport:** Experience the country as locals do, and maybe strike up a conversation with fellow travelers.

✓ **Cycle or Walk:** For shorter distances, consider renting a bike or simply exploring on foot.

5. **Travel Tips:**

✓ **Pack Light:** When on a domestic trip, it's easier to return for items you might have forgotten.

✓ **Try Local Food:** Even within one country, culinary delights can vary vastly from one region to another.

✓ **Respect Local Norms:** Always be mindful and respectful of local customs and practices.

There's a saying, "The beauty of the world lies in the diversity of its people." The same holds true for places. Even within your own homeland, there's so much diversity and beauty to be explored. So, lace up those travel shoes and embark on a journey of domestic discovery!

International Travel

Stepping into a foreign land, with its unique culture, unfamiliar sounds, and intriguing scents, is like opening a new book full of endless stories. The world is vast, and its tapestry of cultures offers an endless array of experiences, each with its own set of lessons and memories.

1. **Embrace the New and Unknown:**

✓ **Cultural Immersion:** Dive into the traditions, cuisines, and festivities of the places you visit. It's the best way to get a real feel of the locale.

✓ **Overcoming Challenges:** Language barriers, unfamiliar customs, or even just navigating new streets can be daunting but also incredibly rewarding when overcome.

2.   **Destination Ideas:**

✓ **World Wonders:** Be it the pyramids of Egypt, the Great Wall of China, or the Northern Lights in Scandinavia, our world is filled with awe-inspiring sights.

✓ **Culinary Expeditions:** Travel the globe through its flavors. From the spicy curries of India to the delicate sushi of Japan, there's a world of tastes awaiting.

✓ **Historical Quests:** Walk in the footsteps of history by visiting ancient ruins, palaces, and landmarks that have stood the test of time.

3.   **Planning Your International Voyage:**

✓ **Research:** Brush up on the do's and don'ts of your destination. A little preparation can go a long way.

✓ **Visas and Documents:** Ensure all your travel documents, including visas, are in order. Always have backups.

✓ **Safety Precautions:** Stay informed about the local safety scenario, especially in unfamiliar territories.

4.   **Getting Around:**

✓ **Local Transport:** Buses, trains, and rickshaws can offer a genuine and often more affordable travel experience.

✓ **Guided Tours:** Opting for tours can help in understanding the local history and context, especially in historically rich regions.

✓ **Walking Tours:** A leisurely walk can often be the best way to discover hidden gems in a new city.

5.   **Travel Tips:**

✓ **Language Basics:** Learn a few essential phrases. A simple "thank you" in the local dialect can open many doors.

✓ **Adaptability:** Things might not always go as planned. Embrace the unexpected.

✓ **Local Etiquette:** Respect local customs, dress codes, and traditions. When in Rome, do as the Romans do!

International travel is more than just sightseeing; it's an education in itself. As you cross borders, you'll realize that while landscapes change, human emotions and dreams remain universal. So, pack that bag, grab your passport, and set forth on a global journey of wonder and enlightenment!

Road Trips and Adventurous Explorations

The thrill of the open road, the changing scenery, and the joy of discovering little-known places, road trips are an adventure in every sense of the word. They're about freedom, exploration, and the stories that unfold along the journey.

1.   **The Magic of the Open Road:**

✓ **The Unknown:** Every turn can lead to a new discovery, be it a charming cafe, a historical landmark, or a breathtaking vista.

✓ **Flexibility:** The beauty of road trips is in the spontaneity. Want to take a detour or linger in a spot a bit longer? You've got the wheel!

2.   **Planning Your Route:**

✓ **Map Out Stops:** While spontaneity is the spirit of road trips, having a rough idea of places to visit can be helpful.

✓ **Safety First:** Ensure your vehicle is in good shape. Pack essentials like a first aid kit, spare tire, and necessary tools.

✓ **Accommodations:** Depending on your style, you can book hotels in advance, camp out, or even opt for quirky stays.

3.   **What to Pack:**

✓ **Snacks and Refreshments:** Stock up on munchies, water, and other refreshments for the ride.

✓ **Entertainment:** Create that perfect playlist, pack some board games or audiobooks for the journey.

✓ **Navigation:** GPS is a lifesaver, but having a traditional map can be both fun and sometimes necessary.

4.   **Road Trip Ideas:**

- ✓ **Historic Routes:** Follow paths that have significant historical importance or take you through old towns.

- ✓ **Scenic Drives:** Opt for roads that meander through landscapes, be it coastal drives, mountain passes, or lush forests.

- ✓ **Thematic Journeys:** Love food? Follow a culinary trail. Passionate about music? Drive from one music festival to another.

5.   **Making Memories:**

- ✓ **Journaling:** Keep a travel diary or start vlogging. It's a way to relive those moments long after the trip.

- ✓ **Photography:** Capture the essence of the journey, not just the destinations but the quirky, unexpected moments along the way.

- ✓ **Meet Locals:** Engage with locals, listen to their stories, and learn about the places from their perspective.

Road trips are not just about the destination, but the experiences and memories created along the way. It's a mosaic of moments, from sunrises witnessed on deserted highways to that surprise rain shower. So, fuel up, roll down the windows, feel the breeze, and let the road guide your adventures!

7.2 Cultural Immersion

Learning Local Traditions

Diving deep into the heart of a place is so much more than just seeing its famous landmarks. It's about immersing yourself in its culture, understanding its traditions, and connecting with its people on a personal level.

1.   **The Joy of Traditions:**

✓ **Deep Connections:** Traditions are the soul of a community. They tell tales of its history, values, and beliefs.

✓ **Shared Experiences:** Participating in local customs lets you be a part of the community, even if just for a short while.

2.   **Where to Start:**

✓ **Local Festivals:** These are a vibrant showcase of traditions. Dance, music, costumes, and rituals, all in one place.

✓ **Traditional Workshops:** Join hands-on experiences like pottery classes in Japan, mask-making in Venice, or rug weaving in Turkey.

3.   **Food and Traditions:**

✓ **Cooking Lessons:** Delve into the culinary heart of a place. Learn to make pasta in Italy, or tamales in Mexico.

✓ **Local Markets:** A bustling hub of activity, local markets offer a peek into everyday traditions. Plus, they're a treat for the senses!

4.   **Engaging with Locals:**

✓ **Homestays:** Living with a local family is the best way to get a genuine experience of their daily life and customs.

✓ **Guided Village Tours:** Local guides can share intimate stories and practices that you might not discover on your own.

5.   **Traditional Arts and Entertainment:**

✓ **Attend Performances:** Be it a Balinese dance, a Maori haka, or an Indian classical music concert, local performances are a window to the heart of a culture.

✓ **Artisan Visits:** See craftsmen at work, be it intricate Moroccan mosaics or the delicate art of Chinese tea-making.

6. **Respect and Open-mindedness:**

✓ **Ask Questions:** If unsure about a local custom or etiquette, it's always good to ask someone knowledgeable.

✓ **Be Respectful:** Always remember you're a guest. Respect local customs, even if they're different from your own beliefs or practices.

When you invest the time to learn and respect local traditions, you not only enrich your own travel experience but also build bridges of understanding and friendship. It transforms travel from being just a 'trip' to a heartwarming, soulful journey.

Culinary and Food Experiences

Ah, the joy of savoring a new dish! Food is not just nourishment; it's an experience, a story of a place and its people, wrapped up in delightful flavors and aromas. When you travel, diving fork-first into the local cuisine can give you insights into a culture like nothing else can.

1. **The Universal Language of Food:**

✓ **Taste Tells a Tale:** Every dish has a story, from the ingredients to the way it's prepared and presented.

✓ **Shared Meals, Shared Moments:** Sitting down to eat with locals can lead to some of the most memorable moments of your travels.

2. **Dive into Street Food:**

✓ **Local Delights:** Street food vendors are often masters of a single dish perfected over years. Try that quesadilla in Mexico City or the pho from a Vietnamese street stall.

✓ **Safety First:** Always choose busy stalls (a sign of fresh produce) and watch how food is prepared.

3. **Fine Dining and Traditional Meals:**

✓ **Elegant Explorations:** Some places offer refined versions of local dishes, letting you explore a culture's cuisine in depth.

✓ **Traditional Feasts:** Look for places that serve traditional set meals, like a Japanese kaiseki or an Indian thali.

4. **Cooking Classes and Workshops:**

✓ **Hands-on Learning:** Roll up your sleeves and learn to cook a dish from scratch. It's a skill you can take home with you!

✓ **Market Visits:** Some classes start with a trip to the local market to pick fresh ingredients, a lesson in itself.

5. **Food Festivals and Celebrations:**

✓ **Taste Galore:** Food festivals let you sample a wide variety of dishes, often with festive music and dance.

✓ **Seasonal Specialties:** Look out for festivals centered around specific produce, like a mango festival or a truffle fair.

6. **Drink in the Culture:**

✓ **Local Beverages:** From sipping sake in Japan to toasting with a glass of Tuscan wine, beverages often have deep cultural roots.

✓ **Brewery and Vineyard Tours:** Understand the process behind your favorite drinks and taste the fresh brews or vintages.

7. **Remembering Through Recipes:**

✓ **Collect Memories:** As you try new dishes, consider collecting recipes. It's a way to relive your travels back home.

✓ **Share and Relish:** Host a dinner themed around your travels. Sharing these culinary treasures with loved ones can be deeply satisfying.

Food is a journey in itself, a delicious exploration of a place's heart and soul. So, on your next trip, let your taste buds lead the way and discover the world one bite at a time.

Interacting with Indigenous Cultures

When we think of traveling, it's easy to list out the famous landmarks or popular tourist spots. But there's an often overlooked depth to exploring, and it lies in understanding and interacting with indigenous cultures. These are the people who've lived on and shaped the land for thousands of years, preserving ancient traditions and stories that can provide invaluable insights into the very essence of a destination.

1. **Genuine Experiences, Not Tours:**

✓ **Beyond Commercialism:** It's essential to approach these experiences with respect and authenticity, not merely as a tourist attraction.

✓ **Seek Authentic Interactions:** Engage in genuine conversations rather than just taking photos or buying souvenirs.

2. **Learning Their Stories:**

✓ **Oral Traditions:** Many indigenous cultures pass down stories orally from generation to generation. Listen, and you'll hear tales of old, legends, and histories that aren't in your typical guidebook.

✓ **Traditional Dances and Songs:** These often narrate stories of their ancestors, nature, or significant events. Participate if invited, but always be respectful.

3. **Respecting Sacred Sites:**

✓ **Holistic Approach:** Understand that for many indigenous cultures, the land, water, and sky are all interconnected and hold spiritual significance.

✓ **Always Ask First:** Before entering a sacred site or taking photos, always ask for permission. Some areas might be off-limits to visitors.

4. **Supporting Indigenous Communities:**

✓ **Purchase Handmade:** Buying locally made handicrafts directly supports the community and helps preserve traditional crafts.

✓ **Engage in Community-led Tourism:** Opt for tours or stays led by the indigenous community itself. It ensures a more authentic experience and that your money goes directly to the community.

5. **Understanding Their Relationship with Nature:**

✓ **Deep Ties:** Many indigenous cultures have a profound connection to the land, viewing it as a living entity to be respected and protected.

✓ **Traditional Knowledge:** They often possess a deep understanding of local flora and fauna, which can be both fascinating and educational.

6. **Participate in Traditional Ceremonies:**

✓ **Unique Insight:** Being a part of ceremonies or rituals can give a rare glimpse into the spiritual and communal aspects of indigenous life.

✓ **Always Be Respectful:** Remember, you're a guest. Follow local customs, dress appropriately, and avoid interrupting or causing distractions.

7. **Leaving with Gratitude:**

✓ **Mutual Respect:** The goal is mutual understanding and respect. Remember to thank the community for sharing their culture and traditions with you.

✓ **Carry the Stories Forward:** Share your experiences with others, but do so with accuracy and reverence. This way, more people can learn and appreciate these rich cultures.

Engaging with indigenous cultures can profoundly enrich your travel experience. It's a journey deep into the heart of a place, led by the very souls who've known it for centuries. But always tread with care, respect, and an open heart, ensuring that these interactions are meaningful and respectful for both you and the communities you visit.

CHAPTER 7 ACTIVITY CHECKLIST

Travel & Exploration

Purpose: Broaden your horizons, experience new cultures, and embark on journeys that enrich your soul.

New Horizons:

- **Domestic Travel:**
  ✓ Choose a city or region in your country you've never been to.
  ✓ Plan a trip: from itinerary to accommodation. Even if you don't go immediately, having a plan is half the fun!
- **International Travel:**
  ✓ Research a country that's always fascinated you.
  ✓ Learn a few basic phrases in the local language. It's always appreciated!
- **Road Trips and Adventurous Explorations:**
  ✓ Map out a road trip route with stops at landmarks or hidden gems.
  ✓ Ensure your vehicle is trip-ready: check tires, fluids, and have an emergency kit.

Cultural Immersion:

- **Learning Local Traditions:**
  ✓ Attend a local cultural festival or event.
  ✓ Try to adopt one tradition or habit from another culture into your daily life.
- **Culinary and Food Experiences:**
  ✓ Visit a foreign restaurant in your hometown or cook an international dish at home.
  ✓ Write down or sketch your favorite meals from your trips for a personal "world cuisine" journal.
- **Interacting with Indigenous Cultures:**
  ✓ Book a guided tour or experience led by indigenous locals.
  ✓ Purchase handcrafted goods directly from indigenous artisans, supporting their community.

Reflective Corner:

1. **Wanderlust Moments:** Share a travel experience that took your breath away.
2. **Cultural Chronicles:** Describe an encounter with a local that gave you a fresh perspective on life.

Bonus Action:

✓ **Travel Journal:** Keep a travel diary. Jot down experiences, sketches, or stick in tickets and postcards.

Note: Every journey, near or far, offers a new story, a new lesson. Embrace the open road and the tales it brings.

Chapter 8:
Relaxation & Mindfulness

"Mindfulness: Because sometimes my mind
is full of... nuts."

Chapter 8: Relaxation & Mindfulness

In today's fast-paced world, finding moments of quiet reflection and relaxation are more crucial than ever. Especially as we move into our golden years, having the tools to manage stress and connect with our inner selves can make all the difference in our overall well-being. This chapter delves into the various techniques and activities that promote relaxation and mindfulness, aiding in reducing anxiety and enhancing our awareness of the present moment. Let's embark on a journey to tranquility and inner peace.

8.1 Stress Reduction

Meditation and Mindful Breathing

Meditation, an age-old practice, has often been touted for its numerous health benefits – both for the mind and the body. And one of the simplest forms of meditation centers around our breath. It's something so inherent and natural to us, yet many of us rarely pay attention to it. Let's dive into this peaceful world.

1. **Basics of Meditation:**

✓ **Find a Quiet Spot:** Begin by choosing a calm and quiet space where you won't be disturbed.

✓ **Comfortable Position:** Whether it's sitting cross-legged, on a chair, or lying down, ensure you're comfortable.

✓ **Close Your Eyes:** This helps to turn your attention inward.

2. **Mindful Breathing:**

✓ **Focus on the Breath:** Pay attention to the inhalation and exhalation, noticing the rise and fall of your chest or the sensation at your nostrils.

✓ **Drifting Thoughts:** It's natural for the mind to wander. When it does, gently bring your focus back to your breath.

3. **Benefits of Meditation:**

✓ **Enhanced Focus:** Regular practice can sharpen your concentration and attention span.

✓ **Stress Relief:** It's a natural antidote to stress, calming the mind and reducing anxiety.

✓ **Emotional Balance:** Meditation can foster a more balanced emotional state and enhance self-awareness.

4.   **Guided Meditations:**

✓ **Assistance for Beginners:** There are numerous apps and online resources offering guided sessions, which can be especially helpful for those new to the practice.

✓ **Variety:** Guided meditations can range from general relaxation to specific themes like gratitude or loving-kindness.

5.   **Incorporate into Daily Life:**

✓ **Start Small:** Even a few minutes each day can make a difference. Over time, you can gradually increase the duration.

✓ **Make it a Routine:** Try to meditate at the same time each day, establishing a habit.

6.   **Breath in Other Practices:**

✓ **Yoga:** Breath plays a pivotal role in yoga, with specific breathing exercises known as 'pranayama'.

✓ **Walking Meditation:** This involves walking slowly and mindfully, synchronizing each step with the breath.

7.   **Final Thoughts:**

✓ **Patience is Key:** Like any skill, meditation requires practice. Be patient with yourself.

✓ **Personal Journey:** Everyone's experience with meditation is unique. It's all about finding what works best for you and embracing the journey.

In this hustle and bustle, taking time to sit with ourselves and our breath is like giving a precious gift to our minds. It's a gentle reminder that amid all the chaos, there's a haven of peace within each of us, waiting to be tapped into.

Yoga and Pilates

When we think about achieving a harmonious blend of mind, body, and spirit, yoga often comes to the forefront. Similarly, Pilates focuses on strengthening the core, enhancing flexibility, and improving overall body alignment. Both practices are not just about physical prowess; they also emphasize mindfulness and connection to oneself.

1. **Yoga: A Journey Inward**

✓ **Origins:** Hailing from ancient India, yoga is a holistic practice intertwining breath, movement, and meditation.

✓ **Different Styles:** From the gentle Hatha and restorative yoga to the more intense Ashtanga or Vinyasa, there's a style for everyone.

✓ **Benefits:** Besides flexibility and strength, yoga can reduce stress, improve respiration, and boost mental clarity.

✓ **Getting Started:** Many communities offer beginner classes, and there are countless online tutorials to help you begin your journey.

2. **Pilates: Core and More**

✓ **Roots:** Developed by Joseph Pilates in the early 20th century, this form of exercise emphasizes postural alignment, core strength, and muscle balance.

✓ **Equipment vs. Mat:** While Pilates can be done on a mat with no equipment, there are also specialized machines like the Reformer which add resistance to the exercises.

✓ **Benefits:** Regular Pilates practice can lead to improved posture, muscle tone, and increased energy.

✓ **Diving In:** Similar to yoga, local gyms and studios often offer classes. Online resources can also guide beginners.

3. **Mindfulness in Motion**

✓ **Breath-Centered:** Both yoga and Pilates put a strong emphasis on breathing, making each movement deliberate and connected to the breath.

✓ **Body Awareness:** As you practice, you become more attuned to your body – recognizing tension, understanding alignment, and acknowledging your limits.

4. **Complementary Practices**

✓ **Together:** While they have distinct principles, combining yoga and Pilates can offer a comprehensive workout regimen that nurtures both the body and mind.

✓ **Balancing Act:** Where yoga emphasizes flexibility and relaxation, Pilates focuses on strength and precision, making them perfect counterparts.

5. **Incorporating into Your Routine**

✓ **Consistency:** Like any exercise regimen, the benefits are most noticeable when practiced regularly.

✓ **Listen to Your Body:** It's essential to recognize your limits and not push too hard. Over time, with patience, your strength and flexibility will naturally improve.

6.   **Community and Connection**

✓ **Join a Class:** Being part of a group class can be motivating and provide a sense of community.

✓ **Retreats and Workshops:** For a deeper dive, consider attending specialized retreats or workshops to further your understanding and skills.

Remember, it's never too late to start. Whether you're a newbie or someone revisiting these practices after a while, both yoga and Pilates offer a welcoming space. It's all about your journey and moving at your own pace. Enjoy the stretch, feel each breath, and cherish the moments of stillness and tranquility.

Spa Retreats and Relaxing Getaways

After the hustle and bustle of daily life, or even the adventures of retirement, sometimes our bodies and minds yearn for a tranquil escape. This is where spa retreats and relaxing getaways come into play. Imagine sinking into a hot tub, having your muscles expertly massaged, or simply breathing in the fresh scent of a serene environment. Sounds tempting, right?

1.   **Why Choose a Spa Retreat?**

✓ **Healing Touch:** Massages, facials, and body treatments not only pamper you but also promote blood circulation, detoxification, and relaxation.

✓ **Mental Reset:** Away from daily distractions, these retreats offer a space for reflection and mindfulness.

✓ **Holistic Wellness:** Many spa retreats integrate wellness sessions, like meditation and yoga, to give a rounded healing experience.

2.   **Types of Retreats:**

✓ **Day Spas:** Perfect for a short break. Get a treatment and spend the day lounging, reading, or dipping in the pool.

✓ **Weekend Getaways:** For when you want a more extended escape but are short on time.

✓ **Destination Spas:** Located in picturesque settings – think mountains, beachfronts, or forests. They often provide week-long programs focusing on complete rejuvenation.

3. **Treatments to Try:**

✓ **Hot Stone Massage:** Warm stones glide over your body, melting away tension.

✓ **Aromatherapy:** Essential oils tailored to your needs, used to enhance mood and promote relaxation.

✓ **Thalassotherapy:** Utilizing seawater and marine products for therapeutic purposes.

4. **Pamper Your Palate:**

✓ **Nutritional Eats:** Many retreats focus on serving wholesome, nutritious meals that complement the healing process.

✓ **Detox Programs:** Freshly squeezed juices and specific foods to cleanse the body.

✓ **Culinary Classes:** Learn to make healthy recipes that you can take home with you.

5. **Choosing the Right Retreat:**

✓ **Budget:** From luxury resorts to quaint bed-and-breakfast spas, there's something for every wallet.

✓ **Focus:** Whether you want a focus on skincare, stress-relief, or detoxification, choose a retreat that aligns with your needs.

✓ **Recommendations:** Always helpful to see reviews or get personal recommendations.

6. **Reaping the Benefits:**

✓ **Lasting Relaxation:** The relaxation you achieve doesn't end when you leave. Use techniques learned to incorporate relaxation into daily life.

✓ **Improved Sleep:** The tranquility of a retreat can help reset your sleep cycle.

✓ **Stress Management:** Learn techniques to manage and reduce stress once you're back in your routine.

Embarking on a spa retreat or relaxing getaway is like hitting the refresh button on a computer. It's about giving your body, mind, and spirit a chance to reset, rejuvenate, and emerge feeling more balanced and vibrant. So, when you're feeling the weight of the world or simply craving some 'me-time', consider a trip to one of these havens of tranquility.

8.2 Daily Mindfulness

Mindful Eating

In our fast-paced world, grabbing a quick bite on the go or mindlessly munching in front of the TV has become the norm. But what if we hit the pause button and truly savored each bite? Welcome to the world of mindful eating, where food is not just fuel but a full sensory experience.

1. **Understanding Mindful Eating:**

✓ **Beyond the Bite:** It's not just about what we eat but how we eat. Being present and fully engaged with each bite.

✓ **Sensory Celebration:** Appreciating the colors, textures, and flavors of our food.

2. **Benefits of Mindful Eating:**

✓ **Digestive Boost:** Taking the time to chew properly can aid digestion.

✓ **Weight Management:** Eating mindfully can prevent overeating by helping us recognize when we're full.

✓ **Enhanced Enjoyment:** Truly savoring our food increases the pleasure of eating.

✓ **Reduced Stress:** Slowing down and being present can have a calming effect.

3. **Tips to Start Your Mindful Eating Journey:**

✓ **Tech-Free Meals:** Ditch the screens and focus solely on your food.

✓ **Gratitude Practice:** Before eating, take a moment to express gratitude for your meal and where it came from.

✓ **Chew Thoroughly:** Aim for 20-30 chews per bite, paying attention to the flavors released.

✓ **Set the Mood:** Create a calm eating environment with dim lighting, soft music, and maybe even some candles.

4. **Mindful Snacking:**

✓ **Quality Over Quantity:** Choose nutrient-dense snacks and savor them.

✓ **Listen to Your Body:** Eat when you're hungry, not out of boredom or emotion.

5. **Dealing with Cravings:**

✓ **Pause Before You Reach:** When a craving hits, take a few deep breaths and check in with yourself. Is it hunger or something else?

✓ **Healthy Swaps:** If you're craving sweets, maybe a piece of fruit will do. Find healthier alternatives to satisfy your cravings.

6. **The Bigger Picture:**

✓ **Mindful Choices:** Think about where your food comes from. Opt for sustainable and ethical choices when possible.

✓ **Shared Meals:** Sharing a meal with loved ones can be a mindful experience in itself. It's about connection, both with our food and each other.

Mindful eating isn't about restriction; it's about liberation. It frees us from mindless habits and opens us up to the joy of truly experiencing our food. So next time you sit down for a meal, take a moment, breathe, and relish every bite.

Mindful Walking

Taking a walk is one of the simplest pleasures in life. But how often do we actually pay attention to each step? Mindful walking is about fully immersing ourselves in the act of walking. It's about feeling the ground beneath our feet, hearing the rhythm of our breath, and truly being in the present moment.

1. **Understanding Mindful Walking:**

✓ **A Walking Meditation:** Mindful walking isn't just about getting from point A to point B. It's a form of meditation where each step becomes a focal point.

✓ **The Journey, Not the Destination:** With mindful walking, the emphasis is on the experience of walking itself, not where you're headed.

2. **Benefits of Mindful Walking:**

✓ **Mental Clarity:** This practice helps to clear the mind and can be a form of moving meditation.

✓ **Emotional Balance:** Connecting with the present can reduce stress, anxiety, and negative emotions.

✓ **Physical Well-being:** You become more aware of your posture, your footsteps, and your body's rhythm.

3.   **Tips to Start Your Mindful Walking Practice:**

✓ **Begin with Intention:** As you start, take a deep breath and set an intention for your walk.

✓ **Focus on Your Steps:** Feel each step as your foot touches the ground and then lifts off again.

✓ **Engage Your Senses:** Listen to the sounds around you, feel the air on your skin, and notice the colors and movements in your surroundings.

✓ **Go Slow:** This isn't a race. The slower you go, the more you can soak in.

4.   **Mindful Walking in Different Settings:**

✓ **Nature Walks:** Connect deeply with nature by noticing the details of the environment around you.

✓ **Urban Mindful Walking:** Even in a bustling city, you can practice mindfulness. Notice the architecture, the blend of old and new, and the multitude of lives intersecting.

✓ **Indoor Walking:** On days when the weather isn't on your side, walk mindfully in a quiet indoor space, like a hallway or large room.

5.   **Group Mindful Walking:**

✓ **Shared Experience:** Walking with a group while practicing mindfulness can amplify the experience. The collective energy can be grounding and supportive.

6.   **Integrating Mindfulness into Daily Walks:**

✓ **Routine to Ritual:** Turn your daily walks, whether it's walking your dog or a simple stroll to the store, into a ritual of mindfulness.

By integrating mindful walking into our daily lives, we open ourselves to a wealth of experiences that often go unnoticed. It's a reminder that there's magic in the mundane and that every moment holds the potential for mindfulness.

• **Mindfulness in Relationships**

Building strong, meaningful relationships is an art. But how often do we take a moment to be truly present with our loved ones? By applying mindfulness to our interactions, we can deepen our connections, understand each other better, and make every shared moment truly count.

1. **The Essence of Mindful Relationships:**

✓ **Deep Listening:** Mindfulness in relationships means truly hearing what the other person is saying without immediately formulating a response or judgment.

✓ **Presence Over Presents:** It's not always about grand gestures. Sometimes, just being fully there for someone is the most precious gift.

2. **Why Mindfulness Matters in Relationships:**

✓ **Boosts Understanding:** When we're present, we can better understand our partner's feelings and perspectives.

✓ **Reduces Conflicts:** Mindful communication can prevent misunderstandings and diffuse tensions.

✓ **Enhances Emotional Intimacy:** Sharing moments mindfully can create deeper bonds.

3. **Tips for Fostering Mindful Connections:**

✓ **Mindful Listening:** Pay full attention when your partner speaks. Avoid interrupting or thinking about your reply.

✓ **Non-verbal Awareness:** Notice your partner's body language. Sometimes, unspoken cues convey more than words.

✓ **Take Breathing Breaks:** If a conversation gets heated, both parties can take a deep breath and come back to the present moment.

✓ **Practice Gratitude:** Regularly express appreciation for the small things your partner does.

4. **Mindful Activities for Couples:**

✓ **Joint Meditation:** Meditate together to share a space of peace and unity.

✓ **Mindful Eating Dates:** Savor a meal together without distractions, cherishing every bite and each other's company.

✓ **Walking Together:** Take strolls and focus on the experience, the surroundings, and the joy of being together.

5. **Overcoming Challenges with Mindfulness:**

✓ **Revisiting Memories:** When facing strains, recall and relive happy memories to rekindle the bond.

✓ **Seeking Mindful Counseling:** Therapies and workshops can introduce couples to techniques that promote understanding and closeness.

6. **Mindfulness with Friends and Family:**

✓ **Stay Curious:** Approach loved ones with a genuine interest, as if you're meeting them for the first time.

✓ **Celebrate Moments:** Be it a small achievement or a simple get-together, be present and make it memorable.

✓ **Limit Digital Distractions:** When spending time together, consider putting away phones to genuinely engage with each other.

By cultivating mindfulness in our relationships, we not only nurture our bonds but also discover the true essence of connection. Remember, it's the quality of time and not just the quantity that shapes beautiful relationships.

CHAPTER 8 ACTIVITY CHECKLIST

Relaxation & Mindfulness

Purpose:

Delve into practices that cultivate inner peace, reduce stress, and promote mindful living in every moment.

Stress Reduction:

- **Meditation and Mindful Breathing:**
✓ Set aside 5-10 minutes daily for quiet meditation.
✓ Practice deep breathing exercises when feeling anxious or overwhelmed.
- **Yoga and Pilates:**
✓ Attend a beginner's yoga or pilates class or find online tutorials.
✓ Dedicate a space in your home for regular practice.
- **Spa Retreats and Relaxing Getaways:**
✓ Book a day at a local spa or wellness center.
✓ Research weekend wellness retreats that resonate with you.

Daily Mindfulness:

- **Mindful Eating:**
✓ Take time to savor each bite during one meal a day.
✓ Reflect on the origins and journey of your food - from farm to plate.
- **Mindful Walking:**
✓ Go for a walk without distractions. Feel every step and observe your surroundings.
✓ Practice gratitude for nature and the beauty it offers.
- **Mindfulness in Relationships:**
✓ Engage in active listening during conversations.
✓ Express appreciation for loved ones regularly.

Reflective Corner:

1. **Peaceful Ponderings:** Share a moment when mindfulness brought clarity or calm to a challenging situation.
2. **Serenity Snapshots:** Describe a setting or experience that epitomizes relaxation for you.

Bonus Action:

✓ **Gratitude Journal:** Every night, jot down three things you're grateful for. Over time, notice the change in your perspective.

Note: Mindfulness isn't about perfection. It's about presence. Celebrate the small moments where you're fully engaged in the now.

HAPPY RETIREMENT

Bucket List

1. FINANCIAL MILESTONES:

Savings Goals:

Short-term Goals (1-12 months)	Long-term Goals (1-5 years)

Use this table to define your short-term and long-term goals. Make sure your goals are (Specific, Measurable, Achievable, and Relevant).

Financial Event to Attend:	Investment Interest:

2. PERSONAL GROWTH & RETIREMENT PSYCHOLOGY:

Retreat or Workshop:

my goals:

Experiences:

Reconnect With:

New Hobby:

GRATEFUL FOR

3. PHYSICAL ACTIVITIES & ADVENTURES:

Physical Activities:

my goals:

Sport/Activity to Try:

Hiking Destination:

Fitness Event/Camp:

GRATEFUL FOR

4.CREATIVE ENDEAVORS:

Art Projects:

my goals:

Workshop to Attend:

Creation Showcase:

Experiences

GRATEFUL FOR

5. LIFELONG LEARNING

Lifelong Learning

my goals:

Course to Enroll In:

Skill to Learn:

Books to Read:

GRATEFUL FOR

6.COMMUNITY & GIVING BACK:

Giving Back

my goals:

Volunteer Opportunity:

Mentorship Area:

Community Event:

GRATEFUL FOR

7. TRAVEL & CULTURAL EXPLORATION:

Cultural Exploration:

my goals:

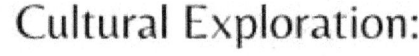

Travel Destination:

Cultural Event/Festival:

Dish to Cook:

GRATEFUL FOR

8. RELAXATION & MINDFULNESS:

Relaxation & Mindfulness:

my goals:

Meditation Retreat:

Unplugged Day at:

Relaxation Space:

GRATEFUL FOR

WORDS OF WISDOM & WELL-WISHES

To:

The journey of retirement is a new chapter, a new adventure waiting to unfold. As you set forth, carry these words with you:

From:

To:

From:

To:

From:

To:

May your retirement be everything you dreamed of and more. Remember the moments we shared, and always know that you have a special place in our hearts. Here's my personal note for you:

From:

To:

From:

To:

From:

To:

From:

To:

From:

To:

From:

To:

From:

To:

From:

To:

From:

To:

From:

To:
_____
_____
_____
_____
From:

To:
_____
_____
_____
_____
From:

To:

From:

To:

From:

To:

From:

To:

From:

To:

From:

To:

From:

To:

From:

To:

From:

To:

From:

To:

From:

To:

From:

To:

From:

To:

From:

To:

From:

To:

From:

AFTERWORD

Ah, dear reader, here we are at the end of our journey together, but truly, this is just the beginning for you. Remember, retirement isn't a finish line; it's the grand opening of one of life's most exciting chapters!

We've navigated the intricacies of finance, delved deep into the realm of psychology, and even flirted with creative endeavors. We've mapped out routes for exploration and ways to embrace a community, all while reminding ourselves of the importance of relaxation and mindfulness. Life after work isn't about winding down—it's about gearing up for a myriad of adventures and opportunities that await.

Now, here's where I ask you a small favor. If this book provided even a glimmer of inspiration or guidance, please pass on the light. Share it with a friend, a family member, or even that neighbor you wave to every morning. Everyone deserves to know that retirement is less about retiring from work and more about refiring one's passions.

Word of mouth is powerful, and recommendations from dear friends, like you, help spread the word faster than you'd believe. Let's collectively shift the narrative and let everyone know that retirement is an exciting new start.

Stay curious, stay active, and most importantly, stay YOU. The world needs the unique gifts that only you can offer, regardless of age. Here's to the golden years being truly golden.

To new beginnings and exciting adventures,

Leon Simonds